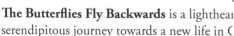

By the same au

A Corfu Trilo

The Butterflies Fly Backwards is a lighthear
serendipitous journey towards a new life in (
catwalks for oilskins and windswept decks, the author had stepped into marital
life in unconventional fashion.
'Charming and amusing in equal measure' Joanna Lumley

The Swallows Fly Back returns to Corfu after a disaster at sea. The author and her
husband take on the challenges of building their new home on the island. Equal
measures of serendipity and calamity help and hinder their best efforts.
'A warm and funny demonstration of the triumph of the human spirit' Julian Fellowes

The Swallows Have Landed charts the family's reversal of fortunes during the
Greek debt crisis and follows them eventually to a tiny granite cottage in Cornwall,
where they must rebuild their lives as best they can.
'Jani writes about Corfu with such candour and affection' Angela Rippon

* * *

A Greek Island Nature Diary

Published by Unicorn
A lavish journal of watercolours of flora, fauna and natural objects found
during the author's years in Corfu and sailing the Ionian. With descriptions of
the medicinal and culinary uses of the wild plants, the book contains personal
observations, smatterings of related Greek Mythology and folklore.
Foreword by John Seymour, Duke of Somerset
Introduction by Dr Lee Durrell MBE

* * *

The Manor House Stories

A series of twelve beautifully produced traditional books for children. These gentle
stories, charmingly illustrated by the author, recount the adventures of a family
of birds and animals who live at the house, recalling the values and traditions of a
gentler way of life that disappeared long ago …
'A wonderful and detailed world in miniature, full of truth and consequence'
– Julian Fellowes

* * *

www.janitullychaplin.com/books
www.themanorhousestories.com

First published in the United Kingdom in 2024 by Jani Tully Chaplin
copyright © Jani Tully Chaplin

ISBN: 978-1-3999-9761-4

Enquiries to: jani@janitullychaplin.com
www.themanorhousestories.com
www.janitullychaplin.com

Printed and bound in the UK by TJ Books, Padstow, Cornwall

Typesetting and design by JS Typesetting Ltd, Porthcawl, Mid Glamorgan
jstypesetting@outlook.com

Cover layout by Rory James Christopher Chaplin, RJCC Events Ltd, Oxfordshire
rjccevents.com

MIX
Paper | Supporting
responsible forestry
FSC
www.fsc.org
FSC® C013056

For Louise ~

Jani Tully Chaplin

2024

The Road to Poor Jesus

Still round the corner there may wait a new road or a secret gate.

JRR Tolkein *The Shores of Faery*

Cover image: La Abubilla, Jésus Pobre
© Jani Tully Chaplin 1987

Contents

Author's note

In this prequel to our Corfu Trilogy I have persuaded Jeremy Just Chaplin to write alternate chapters, giving our personal perspectives on the eventful year we lived in Spain when our children were very young. I am not conceited enough to believe that everyone who opens this book has already read my previous three titles. Nevertheless many will have done so; I can only apologise to them for any repetition necessary in order for others to follow whatever we are banging on about.

Those of you who are familiar with the previous titles will no doubt recognise Jeremy's more orderly style as the polar opposite of my own. In some chapters our reminiscences have necessarily overlapped and we have unwittingly described the same events from our different points of view. At the time of writing, Jeremy and I have been married for forty-four years and, like most couples, our priorities have often been very different; one constant has remained throughout, namely that we wanted to do the very best we could for our children. After four decades our recollections vary in the telling, but Jeremy and I hope you enjoy our combined efforts and leave it to you, dear reader, to choose your corner.

Jani

Preface

Cast your eye over a satellite image of Jesús Pobre today and you may still find traces of the entrancing valley Jani and I stumbled upon thirty-seven years ago. A golf course has long since buried much of the checkerboard orange and almond groves beneath a manicured carpet of greens and fairways, its nearest bunker just five hundred metres from our little finca.

A 5-star hotel and spa now sits, as near as we can tell, below the villa where our friends Roy and Gill once exerted themselves on their private tennis court and entertained us beside their pool. The little tram that occasionally grunted its way sedately through our valley at unknowable intervals has remodelled itself on the Heathrow Shuttle; many of the sinuous dirt tracks have been metalled for the benefit of construction lorries; elderly smallholders have sold their patches of land, their children and grandchildren long since departed for the modern world. The orange trees behind our finca, and away towards the windmills, now lie in untended dereliction except in patches where smart new villas have annexed a grove as a quaint feature. Some gentrification has necessarily taken over the little village, which now finds itself a handy moment's drive from the nearest motorway exit.

Perhaps we and our foreign predecessors at La Abubilla should share a portion of blame for this lost idyll. But our family were merely custodians passing through; we lavished our time and a few pesetas on the finca and left it very much as we had found it. We were most fortunate to live there briefly in such tranquility and it is those perfect months we shall always remember so fondly.

Today, we hear, the little village has reinvigorated itself with the arrival of a less subdued, more adventurous generation that has banished the lingering shadows of Franco and the Civil War. The ancient *riurau* now flourishes as a farmers' and artisans' market – we would have enjoyed that. The tiny Lady Elizabeth School Rory attended is now almost the size of a university. As for the interior design studios and yoga retreats to which every self-respecting village now aspires, somehow we had coped without their presence.

Jésus Pobre is now a different idyll, enjoyed nevertheless by those who have been drawn to it for much the same reason as we had in 1987. We wish them all joy and serenity.

JTC and JJC, North Cornwall 2024

Chapter 1 – Jeremy
The Road Begins

Thus then, o Croesus, man is altogether a creature of accident.

Solon – Athens, 6th Century BC

6th November 1983

The telephone sprang into life a little before three in the morning, its merciless bell piercing my consciousness just as fitful sleep was finally yielding to welcome oblivion after an evening of rare overindulgence. Wretchedly unhappy to be awake, I crawled out of bed into an unfamiliar and inconveniently spinning baby-pink world, which revealed itself inch by inch as my wife's childhood bedroom at her parents' house. Staggering downstairs towards the hall table I fumbled for the receiver, comforting my pounding head with one hand as I tried to make sense of a stranger's voice on the line.

Apparently our house is on fire.

I took a moment to curse the heartless prankster before hanging up and tiptoeing back to our bedroom, intensely relieved to find nineteen-month-old Rory still sleeping peacefully as a dormouse in the travel cot beside our bed. But the telephone renewed its insistent jangling even before I could close the door behind me.

Nature, they say, abhors a vacuum; my own empty head proved no exception and somewhere, as I lurched perilously down the staircase once more, a nagging doubt began to nip at the handful of neurons that were not otherwise engaged in transmitting the throbs of a crashing hangover. Once more I lifted the receiver, its cold bakelite against my ear delivering an involuntary shudder as I listened in ever increasing horror to the caller's vaguely familiar, rich Devonian baritone.

Perhaps this really was the small hours call, seldom a portent of good news, that so many have learnt to dread.

"Young sir, don't you go hanging up on us again! Just listen up a minute: 'tis Kingsbridge Police Station 'ere and your house be afire!" The agitated voice paused briefly enough for an icy chill percolated through the layers of my catatonic stupor. "So you'm best be driving down directly."

A more considerate husband, it was later imparted, would have stirred his wife tenderly from her peaceful slumbers with the muted strains of sitar or harp, accompanied perhaps by the comforting glow of a scented candle, a cup of fresh camomile tea, a salver of lavender shortbread and a gentle neck massage. Instead I decided there was no delicate way of conveying the brutally stark news that our home was ablaze. Running upstairs with racing heart and churning stomach I switched on her bed-side light.

"Wake up, Jani!" I whispered hoarsely, shaking her limp body with immoderate vigour. "Our house is on fire!"

"Oh for pity's sake!" she moaned listlessly, pulling the bed-clothes tightly over her head to banish the unwelcome glare. "Go back to sleep before you disturb Rory; it's just a dream and there's absolutely nothing in the bed."

There was very good reason for her to ignore my entreaties. Not many nights had passed during our honeymoon, some three years earlier, before Jani discovered she had married a crackpot, an outwardly sane, otherwise reserved adult who was occasionally visited by something nasty at the bottom of his bed. Perhaps I should plead my case here.

At the tender age of four I had been attacked by a crab, a colossal cock crab the size of a serving plate, shortly after a Beesands fisherman had placed the motionless carapace of the upturned monster onto my outstretched forearms. How proudly I waded through the deep shingle, staggering under the considerable weight of this unfamiliar prize towards my mother's car … until one giant claw, far stouter than my own puny arms, suddenly lashed out and latched onto the hood of my duffle coat. Swinging itself up like an ape on a climbing frame towards my head, the creature's larger pincer began flailing and snapping menacingly about my face. After several stretched seconds of eternity the fisherman amputated the vice-like pincer from its body with a deft blow from a bagging hook. But the terror of the gnashing pincer and the rasping sibilance of the crustacean's mouth parts and armoured legs, flashing just inches before my eyes, had never entirely left me; instead the childhood memory had plunged deep into my psyche, only to resurface most embarrassingly in the prime of my life.

"CRAB!" I would suddenly howl in the middle of a night, as the recurring nightmare took total possession of my body. "Bloody enormous crab! Get out of the bed NOW!"

Performing a plausible imitation of a demented lumberjack, simultaneously ripping off the sheets and blankets like a chambermaid on piecework, I would rain blows upon our mattress as the monstrous apparition reared up and leveled its massive pincers at me. Then, as Jani gently coaxed me from the nightmare, I would giggle sheepishly and carefully replace the bedclothes, remembering precious little of the episode the following morning. The first time my long suffering wife had witnessed this highly alarming behaviour was on board our catamaran, Aries, the night before we set sail from Falmouth at the outset of our honeymoon voyage to Cyprus. Jani must surely have considered abandoning ship and stealing ashore in the dinghy to summon the men in white coats.

On this occasion however, it was a more measured urgency in my voice that eventually tugged Jani into highly alarmed consciousness. The household apart from little Rory was soon awake as bleary concern quickly turned to stunned disbelief. A thermos of strong coffee was hastily prepared and soon our car was finding its own way through the night with little help from me, winding along the deserted road between the high hedges of the South Hams that had become so familiar to me by daylight and headlight since childhood. Wide awake with caffeine and the second wind that follows interrupted sleep, our mood was darkening from apprehension to indignation. Jani and I were vaguely anxious about the possibility of some minor damage to our freshly refurbished home, yet considerably more determined to discover who or what had started a fire in the first place.

The road between Torbay and Kingsbridge slopped to and fro before my eyes like water in an ocean liner's swimming pool, as we threaded our way along the loose necklace of sleeping hamlets and villages. Startled foxes, badgers and rabbits scuttled away into the penumbra as we passed obliviously through the transient redolences of silage and cowshed, of damp autumn leaves and freshly squeezed pigs.

At last we turned onto the narrow lane that led towards our isolated home and soon found the way ahead blocked by a police car. Beyond, a chaotic fairground of pulsating blue and amber lights illuminated a tunnel of trees overhanging the steep hill. Our home was another half-mile distant, but ominously the air was heavy with smoke.

"You can't drive up yonder," said the policeman, "on account there be fire engines from five different brigades parked up your lane; they'm having to pump water from the creek all the way up over your hill, see. Us spoke earlier, young master; 'tis Gerry Langworthy, your neighbour upalong to Callacombe."

Sure enough the mellow voice I had so recently heard on the telephone belonged to our genial agricultural contractor and part-time policeman, who had known and gently teased me since I was a lad. I started to mouth some words of apology for my offensive telephone manner an hour earlier, but the adrenalin on which I had been running had finally deserted me, confiscating with it all control of my face.

"I did tell 'e of some smoke damage when us spoke on the phone," continued Gerry, shouting above the drone of generators and water pumps as he guided us up the steep lane in the disorientating flicker of lights, stepping carefully over a serpentine tangle of throbbing canvas hoses in the narrow gap between hedge and fire engines. "But it's a tidy bit worse than that now, so you'm best steel yourselves."

"Watch yer language, boys!" came the bluff warning from the chief fireman as we finally raised the brow of the hill and stumbled into the drive of our remote home. "The lady of the house is present."

A huddle of firemen parted like theatre curtains to reveal a scene of utter devastation before us, starkly displayed in arcs of bright halogen from an array of portable floodlights. Nothing could have prepared us for this. A pair of gaunt chimney stacks jutted from jagged piles of smoking debris where our house had once stood, as sporadic eruptions of flame sent showers of sparks high into the darkness above the bowl of light. Random heaps of smoldering furniture, sodden clothes and bedding, all dragged from the inferno by the firefighters, lay scattered about the lawns; however the farthest corner of our home appeared largely intact. I lurched forward to see what might have been spared.

"Steady on now, sir! We're still damping down," warned one of the young firemen, clasping my arm. "Here, one of the lads has made you both some tea."

My default emotion in the face of such adversity had always been blind rage, directed indiscriminately at the whims of fate. For me this fury neatly converted pain into heat, raising the drawbridges around me until I could regain my very English composure; but on this occasion the sight of Jani so utterly distraught was more than I could bear. So we perched uncomfortably on a rockery wall, hugging each other as tears fell into chipped enamel mugs of sweet, treacle dark tea that tasted surprisingly agreeable to a pair of feeble palates more accustomed to weak Earl Grey. Sometimes you must weep to clear your eyes, if only to discern the path ahead.

If there had been worse ways to begin a day, I couldn't actually recall them at the time.

An hour later, with the weapons grade tea still churning in our stomachs, we found ourselves in a bleak interview room at the local Police Station with a rather less sympathetic detective from somewhere up country. He scrutinised us dispassionately with the hollow eyes of a man without a soul as he took down our answers to his questions in assiduous longhand. He noted how we had left our home during the previous afternoon, the 5th November, leaving our tiny son in the capable hands of his grandparents before driving on for supper and fireworks at a friend's house high above the mouth of the River Dart. No, we had not noticed anything suspicious; nothing had been left switched on or lit, apart from a wood burning stove that had been banked up with logs as usual in the forlorn hope that it might stay aglow until our return the following morning.

Our interviews were painstakingly redacted into the stilted vernacular of a formal statement, which we somehow managed to sign through the mists of exhaustion that had so abruptly overtaken us. Another constable, whose shift had just ended, most considerately offered us an early breakfast and the chance of a doze in comfortable armchairs at his own house. More than anything we wanted to go back to Jani's parents, but the young policeman strongly suggested we return to the site at first light. There would likely be looters, he warned, searching the ruins for anything of value that had survived the fire. We could hardly believe our ears. Our appetites had been trapped within knotted stomachs and, impatient to see the worst for ourselves, not an hour passed before we drove back to the ruins of our house in the damp chill of that bleak morning's dawn.

Of the fire engines and teams of firemen there was no trace; only the scattered mounds of unidentifiable wreckage surrounding the pyre remained to greet us. My father's two elderly thoroughbreds – prone to displays of histrionics since he had abandoned them on our land – cavorted along the garden fence beyond, snorting and bucking at the unfamiliar scene and caustic smell before careering pell-mell across the fields and into the rising dusk to repeat the circuit. I urged Jani to stay in the car while I inspected the small corner of the house that was still standing, but she was equally determined to see for herself if any of our possessions could be salvaged. As foretold, I noticed a fresh hole beside the lawn from which Jani's lovingly tended camelia bush had already been uprooted by some heartless, if commendably keen early bird gardener.

Glass crackled beneath our feet as we tiptoed carefully in the half light towards the back of the house, where we gasped at the damage before us. The walls on the farther sides had collapsed, leaving only a skeleton of roof balancing on charred timbers and cracked masonry. Jani was once again in tears as she knelt on the grass next to the shrivelled remains of a Bruce Oldfield evening dress, its contorted black sequins lending it the stiff structure of a snake's shed skin. I tentatively kicked the brittle remains of a door frame, which shivered slightly; when nothing shifted we ventured through, picking our way over the cratered mass of sodden plaster, slates and debris that had collapsed into the void once covered by floorboards and carpets. The acrid smell of our burnt home would never be shaken off.

Miraculously the door to Rory's nursery had been closed when the fire started and it was now the only room with a ceiling over it; nevertheless the little bedroom and its entire contents appeared to have benefited from a signature makeover by Anouska Hempel, armed with her largest canister of black paint. Jani opened the wardrobe and delightedly pulled out an armful of toddler clothes, their bold colours shining out like beacons in the monochrome room. Only later would she discover the invisible, toxic emulsion of vaporised chemical residue that was impossible to shift.

The heat had obviously been intense, yet some obscure corners had quite arbitrarily escaped the worst of the inferno. Hanging over the brittle, charcoaled edge of a windowsill in our bedroom I found a jumbled pile of cassette tapes, all melted, poured and reset like candle wax into a Dali-esque sculpture. The tracks of Led Zeppelin, Steely Dan, Al Kooper, Third World, Abba, Simon and Garfunkel and Cliff Richard albums had been preserved for posterity within a single stalactite of striped plastic – indisputably the only time Jani's gentler taste in music ever fused with my own. Elsewhere sofas and armchairs had been reduced to exposed skeletons of wire coil springs, neatly arranged in geometric patterns on a bed of ash amongst half-consumed webs of withered gossamer. As an art installation the pyre would surely have been shortlisted for one of the pretentious hogwash categories of the Turner Prize, had we the wherewithal to remove it to London.

Dazed by the horror of it all I despaired; but for Jani's sake I tried to remain positive, imagining that somewhere under the soggy rubble a few of our belongings might be recovered. This hope would only be partially redeemed over the following days, as we laboured to sift through tons of clinkers and ash. Eventually we managed to retrieve every carbon coated piece from a canteen of silver cutlery, a dozen or so tar-encrusted crystal goblets, a few ironware pots and pans, and some linen that had been stored with a couple of Jani's summer dresses in an airtight blanket box in the nursery.

Most of my surviving clothes were fit only for the garden shed, to where Jani had often attempted to consign them long before they had gone through the fire. Manifestly the fashion fairy had been re-applying her lipstick when I passed beneath her wand, leaving me to wander through life in a permanent state of unco-ordinated dishevelment.*

Accordingly I refused to part with my best blazer, a generous birthday present from my mother, since it was the only piece of tailoring that had ever contrived to make me appear vaguely presentable; on its rare outings this faithful garment, now more charcoal than navy despite many trips to the dry cleaners, can still to this day set the smoke detectors shrieking in its pungent wake.

Disregarding the contents of our overnight bags at my parents-in-law's house, we possessed little more than the clothes we were wearing. But worse news was to come on the morning of Monday 7th November during a conversation with our insurance company. Unbeknown to me the policy had remained unaltered and unindexed since the day my father had completed the pro-posal form thirty years earlier; accordingly our house was now insured for less than a twentieth part of its rebuilding cost. As if that wasn't serious enough, the total cover for our possessions and household contents would struggle to pay for replacement of the taupe section of Jani's shoe cupboard. Idiotically I had never even bothered to look at the insurance policy I had inher-ited, simply paying the annual premiums without question. I could have kicked myself for being so inattentive, although Jani could willingly have kicked me considerably harder.

But we had been most fortunate, the Chief Fire Officer later insisted, to be elsewhere when the fire had started in the early hours of that morning. In his opinion nobody would have have

---

*Jeremy is the only man I know who never looks in a mirror except to shave, even on the rare occasions he runs a comb through his hair. JTC

escaped from their beds, so rapidly had the fire taken hold. At the time the well known naturalist and broadcaster Tony Soper was one of our closest neighbours a mile or so down the estuary; he had passed along the lane above our home at about eleven that evening and had seen no sign of any fire. In fact the blaze had not been noticed until two in the morning, when a resident across the estuary was rudely awoken by the sound of shotgun cartridges exploding in my gun locker.

* * *

How had we come to such a pretty pass?

My parents Liz and Michael had originally moved to Devonshire in the early 1950's. Almost unnoticed *Horse and Hound* and *Farmers' Weekly* had insidiously joined copies of *Dancing Times* and *Vogue* on the oval coffee table, set beneath the Georgian bow window in the drawing room of my mother's beloved Kensington townhouse. Still trailing the unmistakable aura of his family's lost wealth, Michael had been a sometime impresario and West End theatre manager after the war, although less lyrically he was a singularly unaspiring lawyer with a fatal attraction to racehorses. Not many years had passed since their betrothal before he succeeded in luring Liz away from London, conjuring up an enticing canvas that wove together the verdant rural idyll of Constable's *Flatford Mill* with the wide blue yonder of Millais' *The Boyhood of Raleigh*.

Such a tableau held scant appeal for Liz, who had been a principal dancer with Ballet Rambert until my awkward and weighty arrival put paid to such a demanding regime; yet she could see the benefit for me, barely four years old, in abandoning the fearful smogs and post-war rationing so keenly felt in London.

Any countryside less manicured than Holland Park was entirely foreign to my mother, but she had been suitably mollified by the promised inclusion of Cornish or Devonian coastline within the frame, particularly as she had spent many of her own childhood holidays there in the1920's.

Indeed the farm Michael had eventually stumbled upon far outshone his own utopian fantasy, standing as it did in an exquisite position on the unspoilt western shore of the estuary between Salcombe and Kingsbridge. Its acquisition had been an astonishing stroke of luck. At the time my parents and I (not quite four years old) were attempting to limp home to London from the depths of Cornwall, having just missed the sale of a similar waterside farm opposite Frenchman's Creek on the Helford River. Our progress eastwards had been at a snail's pace, since the radiator of Michael's stately but virtually worthless Derby 3½ required topping up every ten miles; on longer journeys two jerry cans of water could always be seen strapped ignominiously to the running boards, making it the worst example of the aristocratic marque ever to be neglected by its owner. This incontinent relic had finally seized up at the bottom of Kingsbridge hill, whence, still sporting its wartime livery of brush painted camouflage, it was ignominiously towed away. Only the most outlandish of serendipities could have thrown us into the path of our rescuer, namely the genial land agent who the very same morning had taken instructions on the farm that would become our home for the next twenty-six years.

Michael had carefully glossed over several considerable drawbacks to the outwardly elegant, provincial Georgian farmhouse. Liz would not discover the lack of electricity, running water, heating and telephone, nor even ceilings and floors with any vestige of structural integrity until it was too late for her to scoop me up and retreat to Kensington; I had thought it a wonderful adventure when a joist gave way in the middle of our first night at the farm, nearly sending me and my little divan bed into the dining room below. Very soon my mother would also learn that Michael, being Michael, expected her to stump up for all repairs and improvements to the house out of her own capital, not to mention a herd of pedigree Jersey cattle, a new Dutch barn, two tractors and a full complement of farm implements – none of which came cheap.

To their friends, unsurprisingly, my parents' decision to settle in this cultural exile amidst the bucolic wilds of Devon, so far removed from their previous lives, seemed more than a trifle absurd. But to me, as a four year-old whose adventures had hitherto begun and ended at the Round Pond in Kensington Gardens under the watchful eye of my nanny, the hundred acre farm was a revelation. With its array of musty barns and hay lofts, its thorn entangled piles of wondrous, obsolete horse-drawn machinery, my new home was an endless paradise beyond compare. Better still, the farm's half-mile frontage to the estuary would in time provide me with the means to get afloat in canoes and sailing dinghies from the age of seven.

The decades flew by, the farm had eventually been sold and in May 1980 Jani and I were married, having fallen in love after knowing and periodically dating each other for fifteen years. The pair of labourers' cottages that would become our first marital home had once been part of the farm and stood in their own glorious twenty acres of land. Six weeks after our wedding Jani and I had cast off from the mooring below our fields on an extended honeymoon to Cyprus aboard our first catamaran, *Aries*.

I had been able to buy the boat with the proceeds of a small inheritance from a great aunt; more by luck than judgement I had invested the bequest in a property that doubled its value within the space of three years.

This might all sound hideously elitist, but it's worth remembering that many council house tenants would also be sailing away into the sunset before long, having profited massively from Thatcher's 'Right to Buy' policy – we met several of these born again adventure capitalists over the following years. Far from an extravagance, we lived very comfortably on the island for the princely sum of thirty pounds a week, easily paid for by Jani's lucrative modelling work in the fashion world and by my less regular work as a delivery skipper. Two years later we reluctantly sold Aries and bade a sad farewell to Cyprus, returning home in time for our son's birth.

Back in Devon our pair of cottages had been let during the two summers of our absence afloat in the Mediterranean. The laborious and expensive business of modernising and uniting them into one larger family home, financed by the proceeds of our catamaran's sale in Cyprus, had been well under way when the fire struck. Freshly confronted with the realities and responsibilities of parenthood it had been a rude awakening to find ourselves so suddenly homeless, stripped of all the treasured mementos, possessions and wedding presents that marked out the three years of our marriage. At the time the fire seemed like a crushing setback; moreover we felt unjustly persecuted when it transpired the blaze had most probably been started by a local arsonist. Our particular pyromaniac was a disturbed and disadvantaged young man who eventually took his own life after being implicated in a spate of similar fires, one of which consumed his own father.

My young family's destiny had been altered in a flash; but not, as events would conspire, altogether for the worse.

* * *

The local newspapers each put their own inimitable slant on our misfortune. Relegating their usual headlines about prize-winning pumpkins to the inside pages, one banner, REMOTE COTTAGE INFERNO BLAMED ON WATER, referred obliquely in its Devonian way to the lack of any fire hydrant within a country mile of our home. Instead the resourceful firemen had pumped water up our steep hill from the nearest creek – a method that had eventually extinguished the fire, but had also soaked any surviving household contents with very muddy salt water. The banner might have lacked the iconic status of my mother's favourite unintentional wartime headlines, such as the comical EISENHOWER FLIES BACK TO FRONT, or the easily misunderstood BRITISH PUSH BOTTLES UP GERMANS; nevertheless we kept several copies of the idiotic rag's front page as souvenirs of a lighter moment from that gloomy period.

Our home might well have been modest, but the site upon which it stood was a flawless gem, sitting at the head of the valley above our private foreshore and tumbledown quay. A decade earlier two dividing hedges of majestic English elms traversing the valley of wild pasture had been decimated by the Dutch elm beetle; as the screens of branches and ivy clad trunks were cleared, so the extraordinary prospect over meadow and water had been fully revealed. I vowed that with Jani's support I would build a new house on this exquisite site with my own bare hands; after all, if the average builder could master a trade or two, then so indeed could I.

The small matter of finances presented a significant hurdle, but when the news came that our insurers had agreed to settle the claim in full – however paltry that was – Jani and I felt confident enough to engage an architect who we knew slightly. While we bickered with the blinkered planning authorities, who were determined we should replace our old home with something closely resembling a municipal toilet block, the next few weeks were spent poring through library books on all manner of subjects from the technicalities of foundation laying, roofing, plumbing and electrical installation, to drain design, door hanging and central heating. But in truth the skills gained on the farm during my youth had already turned me into a dexterous old bod. For my sins I had spent many a summer afternoon crawling with a set of spanners into the sweltering belly of a combine harvester, many a dark winter morning replacing frozen valves in the dairy's serpentine milking machinery, and many a month patching up the farm's much neglected barns.

My instructors had been our unlettered yet solidly wise farmhands, the humble men who had never ventured north of Totnes except in service of their country as stokers on the merchant ships of the valiant North Atlantic convoys. On the farm they ate well and lived rent free in our cottages, but even as a young boy I noticed how their labourers' wages were reflected in the sackcloth they wore; as winter bit harder, so the number of sacks on their backs and around their waists increased until they resembled rotund, walking bales of jute. (Their parsimony was a lifestyle choice, a fierce frugality hammered into them through generations of their downtrodden, God fearing forebears. When one of them died in 1972 a horde of cash was discovered in his mattress; his son was dumbfounded to count up over twenty thousand pounds – the price of two houses at the time.) Monosyllabic as they were, no text books could ever have imparted their practical skills and knack for lateral thinking and improvisation, which crueler minds might call the noble art of bodging.

In a perfect world the local planning authorities would have preferred no building of any description to be erected at the head of our beautiful valley. I got the distinct impression they were spinning out the application process in the hope we might abandon the idea of rebuilding altogether; but in fact one of the many idiocies of planning law would have allowed us to build an enormous Dutch barn on the site without any permission whatsoever. I seem to remember threatening to erect such an eyesore at one of our many hostile meetings. Our skirmishes with the planning officer were further aggravated by our architect, who had made an art of baiting the wretched official over the years. At a preliminary meeting he had conjured up a set of outline plans for a colossal rotunda in the Palladian style – somehow managing to keep a straight face throughout – explaining how he expected our new house to be a grand statement, an edifice with a copper-clad dome that would strike a blow for mediocrity and be visible from space.

Unfortunately our architect was rather too convincing for his own good and the planning officer swallowed the implausible fabrication completely. Our relationship with this man deteriorated further when Jani became incensed with the man's obsession with the lowest common denominator where local architecture was concerned. Eventually tempers calmed, allowing a compromise to be reached and our plans to be approved. The drawings showed a long, low building with overly generous eaves to provide some shade to the acres of glass that made the most of our extraordinary views. Jani and I had given our architect a very detailed brief and he had drawn the plans accordingly, incorporating a staircase leading to a mezzanine level with an office and a long balcony overlooking the sitting room.

My first task was to clear the tons of combustible debris from the site. This was going to be a costly and time consuming endeavour, until I quickly hit upon a far simpler plan to short circuit the process: I would simply set fire to the remains. On the appointed day, after alerting the County Brigade Headquarters and the local Fire Station to my intention to start a controlled fire, I struck a match and tossed it into the mountainous pile of paraffin-soaked timbers and rubble. As a man who regularly struggled to light a barbecue I was still dubious about my skills as a firebug, but my success was astonishing and within minutes the entire site was ablaze. Flames leapt fifty feet into the sky, reaching out greedily as the gusting wind sent hungry tongues of fire licking this way and that. Thick palls of smoke soon fanned down our valley and hurried like startled ghosts over the estuary, immediately alerting the good people of West Charleton to my deliberate but barely controlled fire. Moments later the unwelcome sound of distant fire sirens drifted across the water and up the valley, rising inexorably to a crescendo ten minutes later as the first of three fire engines wheezed its way over the crest of the hill and pulled into our drive. Fortunately the blaze had already passed the height of its intensity and, as the soaring flames subsided, the firemen withdrew in considerable animosity despite my most abject apologies and protestations. By teatime all that remained of our home was a surprisingly small pile of blackened stone and brick, which was easily bulldozed into the contours of the flattened site.

A few days later Jani brought Rory over to visit for the first time since the house had burnt down, never imagining for a moment that a toddler of nineteen months would recognise the site where his home had once stood. Rounding the corner of the drive Rory drew himself up stiffly in his pushchair, raising an arm to point a pathetically quivering finger towards the barren, featureless earth.

"Home?" he inquired plaintively.

Jani and I feared our son might be scarred for life, but as the years passed we came to see this wide-eyed imitation of ET was merely the first manifestation of a mischievous humour and mastery of pathos. Amidst our anguish the red Devonian earth had thrown a cathartic shroud over the cremated ashes of our dwelling; and in the dim distance ahead we could just discern the first faint glimmer of a silver lining, even if it remained stubbornly stitched to a thundercloud.

Fortunately youth and resilience were still on our side.

Chapter 2 – Jani
Every Cloud...

It's best to have failure happen early in life.
It wakes up the Phoenix bird in you so you rise from the ashes.

Anne Baxter

Overnight Jeremy and I found ourselves homeless with a toddler to look after. Naturally we were welcomed with open arms by my parents, who adored having us to stay in the pale pink bedroom of my childhood. They were so in love with Rory, and he with them, that they never wanted us to leave. But Jeremy needed to be as near as possible to our land and the charred ruins of our former home; Torbay was too far for daily journeys and he was anxious to start rebuilding a home for us as soon as planning permission was granted. We fully anticipated this would be a straightforward process leading to a foregone conclusion; after all, the former farmworkers' cottages had been there for the best part of a century before Jeremy's parents converted them into holiday lets. Liz had extracted the humble cottages and their twenty acres of land from her reluctant husband as part settlement for the money she had spent to improve the farm all those years earlier, whereupon she had most generously gifted them to us on our marriage in 1980.

We immediately enlisted the help of a young architect of our slight acquaintance who was eager for work. With Rory blissfully happy to be entertained by his doting grandparents, we arranged a meeting in a café in Kingsbridge, where we outlined a vague plan for the house we hoped to build as we sipped our coffee.

I grabbed a paper napkin and drew a very rough sketch with a biro as Jeremy described his ideas for the roofline and balconies, much in the style of an Andalusian hacienda. We wanted to take full advantage of the stunning views from the front aspect, which led the eye over our valley to the estuary beyond, thence to the tiny hamlets nestling in the rolling hillsides far away on the opposite side; this fabulous vista warranted floor to ceiling windows and French doors throughout. My rough sketch looked surprisingly attractive and our architect tucked it into his briefcase, promising to arrange a site meeting with the local planning officer as soon as possible. Jeremy might have preferred a more traditional design, but Georgian windows, however large, could never do full justice to the views.

Our architect decided to stay away from our first site meeting, having already upset the unfortunate official quite enough during previous encounters. In his absence Jeremy and I had hoped to smooth ruffled feathers and were in optimistic mood until we actually met the planning officer, a disappointing man in a shabby cagoule, whose mean expression betrayed a loathing for anyone more fortunate than himself. He was the sort of man who didn't notice women, speaking only to Jeremy as I attempted to point out the remoteness and relative invisibility of our site.

"What sort of house did you have in mind?"

"Ah, yes ..." Jeremy faltered as he framed a suitably tactful answer.

"We'd like something resembling a traditional Spanish farmhouse," I jumped in cheerily, carefully substituting alternatives for the more attractive *Andalusian* and *alquería*, which he might not have understood.

"I can safely say that would never be passed," he replied with relish, as he deigned to look at me for the first time. "And you've only got six months before you lose all rights to rebuild, so I suggest you opt for something very ordinary."

My blood began to boil at this point; it was *our* land after all. How dare this puffed up official dictate what sort of home we should build on our own land.

"Well, what sort of very ordinary house *would* be passed without opposition?" I asked, failing to keep the dripping sarcasm from my voice.

"Have you seen the new houses above the industrial estate in Kingsbridge?" he asked.

"Do you mean those depressing grey concrete boxes with windows smaller than postage stamps?" I replied, as Jeremy's face turned ashen.

"Yes, that's it. Put in a plan like one of those and it should be passed straight away. It has to be something that wouldn't upset the neighbours."

"Now you really are joking," I laughed, nudging him gently on the shoulder, as Jeremy kicked my ankle.

"But we don't have any neighbours," reasoned Jeremy, "and it will be invisible from the far side of the water without a telescope!"

"Yes, but people coming up the river might see it," he asserted, as my Arian horns popped out. I simply couldn't help myself.

"So are you telling us to build something that wouldn't offend any passing yachtsmen?", I squealed as Jeremy tugged at my arm. "And are you presuming these sailors would prefer to see something that resembles a municipal toilet block, as you so obviously would?"

"Well you've done it now!" Jeremy fumed as the man scuttled away towards his car. "You've put his back up and we'll probably be denied permission for anything at all!"

Terrifyingly Jeremy was right. The final decision would rest on this man's recommendation. Our architect's revised plans followed our brief, although I did have to insist on a change to one of the rooms. A long galley style kitchen opened into a spacious eating and sitting area with huge floor to ceiling windows and French doors leading out onto terraces and gardens. But only a man could have made the mistake of designing a kitchen without windows, ('Well, you won't want to be distracted when you're washing up or cooking'). This was quickly rectified and a large window was added on either side; one looked over the courtyard and the sweeping drive to the lane above, the other framing the matchless view over our valley and estuary beyond. From the kitchen sink I would now be able to see who was coming down the drive to visit us; whilst at the cooker I could gaze at our ponies grazing in the top field and at any passing craft on the water below.

Thankfully our less ambitious planning application was passed relatively quickly and Jeremy began to prepare the ground for the new foundations. He had quickly realised he would have to do all the work himself, since the meagre insurance money and our equally meagre resources would not allow for professional builders or other tradesmen. In the meantime we had found somewhere to rent until our new home was ready; its adequate accommodation formed the upper floors of a picturesque boathouse on the farther side of the river; most handily it was directly opposite our land. There were three bedrooms and a large sitting room with a long balcony jutting above the foreshore below, which of course disappeared at high tide. Its furnishings dating from the 1950's were decidedly tired and depressing, but the position and views more than compensated for such drawbacks.

The boathouse directly beneath us had slatted doors to allow the highest tides to wash in unimpeded; during periods when high water coincided with stormy weather the dinghies therein would knock together noisily like dodgem cars until the tide fell. Whenever a gale blew directly upriver the frightful thin carpets, all of them chocolate brown flecked with purple and black, would rise up like the fabric of an inflating hot air balloon as the draught whistled through the cracks between the floorboards. Walking across the sitting room in these conditions involved lifting up our feet as if we were attempting to climb a staircase in a pair of flippers.

Such a wonderfully well ventilated house was impossible to keep warm in winter, but in the summer months it was a delight. I could see Jeremy's Land Rover parked in the far distance over the estuary and would prepare lunch as soon as I spied him leaving the site; in the evenings he never left until the light began to fade, which made for some very long summer days' work. After supper he read guides and specification sheets on whatever materials were required for use the following day – there certainly wasn't much time for smalltalk during those eighteen months. Of course there were no mobile phones in the 1980's, so we relied on a primitive form of semaphore if we needed to communicate – both of us with binoculars at the ready.

I will never forget the day I saw Jeremy frantically waving at me with an old red towel. I bundled Rory into his car seat and drove round the head of the estuary to the site, where we found Jeremy, evidently in great pain, sitting on a pile of concrete blocks with a short wooden plank attached to his foot. He had jumped down from a trestle and landed on an offcut of timber that happened to have a six-inch nail sticking out of it; the spike had harpooned his boot and embedded itself securely between the middle bones of his foot. Desperately trying to stifle my giggles at such an absurd spectacle I eventually got him loaded into the back of the Land Rover. With his foot, complete with plank, hanging out of the tailgate I drove him to the local cottage hospital – I don't remember which half-witted health minister it was who closed them all – where the nurses queued up to marvel (and titter) at the unusual injury. Health and safety had never featured high on my husband's agenda.

During the summer months I had to keep the doors leading to the balcony permanently open, as the little boathouse absorbed the heat and held it until late into the night. This presented a problem with Rory, an energetic and inquisitive little boy, who had begun to walk at ten months; no cupboard, shelf or electricity socket was safe from his curiosity by the time we got to the boathouse. I couldn't take my eyes off him for a moment to cook or clean after he awoke at dawn and thereafter wanted to be occupied. I usually ran out of ideas by nine in the morning; even vacuuming was out of the question, for he couldn't stand the noise and would run to the plug and pull it out of the wall as soon as I switched it on. Rory quickly developed a fetish about plugs: they were pulled out and pushed back in again without the slightest regard for the timers on our video recorders and alarm clocks, which had to be reset daily. Perhaps Jeremy and I should have guessed Rory would one day have a vast warehouse full of sound and lighting equipment with several miles of cables and thousands of plugs and sockets, for his own events company. No matter how much I scolded him, he would just grin at me and repeat the process. With Jeremy absent from dawn to dusk I had virtually become a single mother and I soon decided it was time to put an advertisement in the local press for a 'Mary Poppins'. At eight o'clock sharp on the morning it appeared in the newspaper I took a phone call from a young woman who sounded perfect. Kim was married to a farmer from Slapton and she immediately solved the problem of hoovering. She simply hoisted Rory onto one ample hip and carried him indefatigably around the house, hoover in the other hand. Rory adored her from the first day, but as he always associated her with the hoover – haboo in Rory's toddler language – Kim also became 'Haboo'.

Three months before his second birthday I enrolled him in the pre-school playgroup, held once a week in a quaint village hall of a tiny hamlet nearby. It was run by a kind, homely Devonian lady who enjoyed sitting next to Rory at the long table as he fiddled about with playdough or plasticine, chatting to him about all sorts of things. As the weekly sessions progressed, I noticed the other lady helpers would choose to do the same, but they didn't sit with any of the other children whose mothers, like me, had to be present. One morning at break time I got to the bottom of this, when one of the helpers said they all liked to sit with Rory because they couldn't believe how he could engage in a conversation as easily as a much older child. It hadn't really occurred to me until then, but I put it down to the fact that all his family had talked to him constantly from the day he was born; and from six months he was read a bedtime story, usually Beatrix Potter, every night in his cot.

Admittedly I never enjoyed those weekly sessions as much as my young son, especially the compulsory singing to such favourites as *The Wheels On The Bus, Old Macdonald Had A Farm* and *I'm A Little Teapot*. Mothers, children and helpers had to sit on the dusty wooden floor and were all expected to do the movements as well as sing, which always made me feel very self-conscious. The sight of the rotund lady organiser in a flowery dress enacting a teapot, with one arm bent at the elbow like a handle and the other outstretched, hand pointing downwards like a spout, tipping herself back and forth in time to the song made me want to burst out laughing every time. Rory called her 'Mrs Teapot' and to this day neither of us can remember the dear lady's real name.

I had another reason to feel embarrassed during these playgroup days. All the other mothers, children and helpers were invariably dressed in comfortable, well worn clothes, which was a very sensible idea given that young children and messy play were involved. However the only clothes Rory and I had were brand spanking new, since all our clothes had been destroyed in the fire. One morning Mrs Teapot announced, looking pointedly at me, that everyone should wear *old* clothes the following week as we would be off for an outing to the nearby beach. I felt I had to say something. After the others had left, I approached Mrs Teapot and explained that Rory and I only had new clothes because all our others had been lost in the fire. Her look of astonishment turned to one of compassion; she enfolded me in a suffocating bear hug to her ample bosom as Rory watched wide eyed, waiting for me to reappear.

She must have told the other helpers about our situation, because they were extra kind to both of us thereafter; they even made sure I was given one of the special chocolate biscuits reserved for the helpers at break time. I daresay they had been telling each other there was absolutely no need for us to show off by arriving each week in clothes that were so obviously brand new.

During the months after we returned from living in Cyprus, I had joined the ante-natal classes at our local GP's surgery in Salcombe. I was seven months pregnant with Rory and felt it might be a good idea to learn something about childbirth, although I soon decided ignorance might have been the less traumatising option. Jeremy thoughtfully bought me *Baby & Child* by Penelope Leach which was lauded as being the best and most informative book on parenting at the time. Dutifully I ploughed through the chapters on giving birth (which made me want to bury my head in the sand) but when I reached the part about potty training I couldn't quite believe what I was reading. The expert Penelope advocated allowing the child to 'play with its own faeces in the potty', her reasoning being that if you showed the slightest disgust, the child would think that if you were repulsed by what they had just produced, you were repulsed by them too. When I shrieked in horror and read this aloud to Jeremy, he grabbed the book and threw it into the dustbin. A girlfriend of mine suggested I would learn everything I needed to know from the National Childbirth Trust of which she was an enthusiastic member. I duly joined a local class and sat patiently listening to their advice regarding childbirth. Much emphasis was placed on breathing, sucking ice cubes, gas and air, 'thinking away the pain' and when to push. I put up my hand and asked why they weren't mentioning epidurals, which is what I was definitely having. Gasps of disapproval filled the room and I was firmly told these were not available on the NHS.

When I explained I was a private patient and my gynaecologist had already booked in the day I would be painlessly delivered of my baby, along with the anaesthetist who would administer the epidural injection, you could feel everyone's hackles rise and black looks were directed towards this wimpy mother-to-be. I left in silence and never returned, from then on referring to the organisation as the National Childbirth Torturers.

Two of the other expectant mothers and the young midwife who took the classes at the Salcombe clinic became lifelong friends. Sue had just returned from Germany where her husband, an army helicopter pilot, had been stationed for two years. Lindsey and her husband lived in Kingsbridge and we were all expecting our babies around the same time. I was mightily amused and impressed that our pretty and vivacious auburn-haired midwife, Margaret, who was also expecting, wore bright red underwear beneath her neat blue and white nurse's uniform, as many of our floor exercises easily revealed. Months later, when Jeremy and I were living at the boathouse, these three young mums and I met regularly and it was not long before I instigated a plan to give us all a bit of much needed free time from our toddlers. Every Wednesday afternoon one of us would look after the other three children at our own home, thus giving each mother three Wednesday afternoons of freedom and sanity every month. The system worked brilliantly and I think my session was the easiest because I took them all down to the foreshore where the children could run free, make mud pies, gather shells and paddle in their rubber boots. I would then give them snacks before their mothers collected them, in soiled condition, at four o'clock.

So far so good, until one afternoon when my three friends

came to collect their daughters as usual. We said our goodbyes and they made their way up the steeply winding path to the main road where they had parked their cars. Rory and I waved them off and had just shut the front door when we heard a deep rumble that made the house shake, instantly followed by an almighty crash and the sound of rocks hitting the front door. It sounded like an earthquake. I pulled Rory further back into the sitting room and out onto the balcony, terrified the sheer cliff, towering thirty feet above our front door, was about to collapse completely and carry the house away. I wrapped Rory in a warm coat and carried him down the wooden steps from the balcony to the beach, where I thought we would be safe until Jeremy came home. As it was winter he returned from the building site a few minutes later and made his way down the path in total darkness.

Imagine his horror at being confronted by a hillock of rock and rubble blocking the front door, completely burying the steps that led to it. Some of the boulders weighed over a ton each and were far too heavy for Jeremy to shift until he could break them up, so the beach became our only approach for the next few days. If the landslide had happened a minute earlier, when my three friends, their little daughters, Rory and I had been chatting and saying our goodbyes, we would all have been squashed flat like a family of frogs on the road.

As the weeks sped by I could see our new home growing brick by brick, rising like a Phoenix from the ashes. My days with Rory followed a steady and enthralling routine; shopping for food became my daily exercise, for there was little storage space and only one tiny fridge at the boathouse. I would bundle Rory into his pushchair, puff up the steep path to the main road and walk the fifteen minutes into Kingsbridge. The grocer's shop was on the level at the top of the town, where I would buy my fresh vegetables and fruit and hang the bags onto the handles of the buggy. On more than one occasion I overloaded it and the weight of the bags caused the pushchair, with Rory strapped in, to topple onto its back; luckily Rory just laughed and enjoyed the ride, cushioned by potatoes, oranges and cabbage. But all the other shops I needed were situated on either side of the very steep main street, where access was up three or sometimes four dangerous steps from the impossibly angled pavement; in the years we lived there, not a single shopkeeper or assistant offered to help lift the pushchair into their shop. I began to hate them all.

(Three years later, on the day before we were about to leave England for Spain, I had to collect an order from one of these inhospitable shops.

"Name?" asked the lady, as she always did.

I saw red. Within days of our arrival in Cyprus at the beginning of our two year honeymoon, every Greek Cypriot shopkeeper in Larnaca had learnt and remembered my name; and what's more they delighted in getting to know us better, thereby winning our loyal custom with their irrepressible affability. The lady who owned the haberdashery shop even told me I was expecting a baby before I had realised myself, just three weeks in to my pregnancy!

"I've been coming here at least once a week for the last four years," I fumed, "and still you can't be bothered to remember my name, even though I know yours, and this is just one of the many reasons I will be so delighted to leave England!"

There was no audible response from her blank face as I stormed out empty handed, mentally noting yet another good reason for leaving Devon to its matchless customer service.)

On fine days I would take lunch to the building site, where the three of us would enjoy a picnic sitting in the back of the Land Rover or on a rug in the garden. My parents would often come down and take Rory to Bantham or Bigbury where he would be in heaven, making sandcastles with my father and tucking into a sumptuous picnic lunch brought by his adoring Granny. Sometimes I would leave Rory at my parents' house for the day, although he was never a good traveller and was frequently carsick during the hour's drive in my elderly MG Midget. I had a terrifying experience on one of these journeys. Suddenly on a blind corner before Totnes I heard the voice of a former boyfriend as clearly as if he was sitting right behind me.

"Slow down, Pussycat!" warned the familiar voice of the man who had died the year before.

I was so shocked I immediately took my foot off the accelerator and slowed to a crawl beside the hedge as an enormous pantechnicon careered around the bend in the middle of the road. I screwed up my eyes and waited for the impact, hearing the blast of a horn and the squeal of tyres before opening my eyes in time to see the lorry's wheels missing us by inches as it flashed past me. I managed to crawl as far as a small lay-by ahead, where I sat shaking for an eternity before I felt composed enough to continue my journey. Nobody will ever convince me we don't have guardian angels.

Jeremy had spent a fortune having my Midget fully restored, in fact there was nothing left of the original 1962 body after the garage had stripped away the rusty panels, (including all the gaping holes I had attempted to fill with wire wool pan scourers.) Then, shortly after Miranda was born, he caught me as I was about to drive away with Rory in the passenger seat and Miranda in her carrycot balanced on the back shelf. Jeremy insisted I never drove it again with the children, which in practical terms meant it had to be sold. He was right of course; I hadn't realised how fantastically dangerous it was. Whenever I see a Midget nowadays I simply cannot believe how incredibly tiny and low to the ground it was, scarcely bigger than a go-kart. But it was the easiest car to park in the tightest of spaces.

I couldn't be of much practical help to Jeremy on the building site until the decorating stage; he was doing everything single-handed, even lifting heavy lintels one end at a time with levers, but he did ask me to help him level the concrete floor of the double garage. Two people were essential for this job, one on each end of the tamping beam (a very long baulk of wood with handles at either end, used for levelling wet concrete to form an even surface). As we waded slowly through the gloopy mixture from one end of the garage to the other, Jeremy seemed pleased with the results and I was equally delighted to have been of some practical use at last ... until the next morning, when I discovered that my dear husband had forgotten to wash the wet cement from my expensive Hunter wellies. They had dried hard, set like a pair of grey concrete garden ornaments and useful only as planters thereafter.

By the time Rory was two and a half the new house was almost complete. Haboo had left us to help her husband with a straw-berry growing enterprise and Rory was enrolled in a small Nursery School near Thurlestone, where he went for two mornings each week. My parents had since moved from Torbay to Thurlestone to be closer to us; handily the Nursery was opposite this new home and they could wave to Rory from their garden. He loved being met by them at lunchtime and taken to their house for the afternoon. This gave me much needed time to concentrate on creating a garden around our new house; the local garden centres did very well out of me during that summer. Jeremy had made a marvellous job of the building work, although plastering the walls and ceilings was a skill too far and required the employment of professionals. His most exhausting task concerned the roof. Our hope of using traditional Spanish terracotta roof tiles had been knocked on the head by the anoraks in the local planning department, who had stipulated English concrete tiles instead – much to our disgust. Nearly 3,000 of them were needed and each tile weighed five kilos, so he could only carry four at a time repeatedly up the ladder to the roof. He was remarkably fit and short tempered by the end of it.

I had loved the farm cottages from the first time I went to stay there as Jeremy's fiancée, although of course I had also stayed at Liz and Michael's Georgian farmhouse, only seven fields away, when I was just fourteen. Being a horse mad teenager I had been thrilled when Jeremy's father, who at long last having found someone who shared his passion for horses, had taken me to the paddocks to see his jet black thoroughbreds. Jeremy and his mother, as well as all the farmhands wouldn't go near them; the local vets were equally petrified by their antics and drew straws to see which partner would have to visit the farm to treat them. I had taken no notice when Jeremy first warned me never to enter their paddock to say hello to two of these handsome youngsters, but I soon wished I had. Careering towards me in turn before wheeling round at the last moment, they lashed out with their hind legs, bucking with a lethal intent I had never seen in any horses before. The sire of all Michael's racehorses had savaged and killed his groom in a stable, so it was only to be expected that his progeny all turned out devilishly jet black and equally *un*stable. Most of these thoroughbreds failed miserably on the racecourse, but one of Michael's rejects was sold for a pittance and went on to win the Ridden Show Hack Class at the Horse of the Year Show in London. I wish I'd been around then to show him myself.

The genetic delinquency in these horses had gradually spread a contagion of unpredictability around the farm. Jersey heifers, usually so placid, often charged at anyone foolish enough to stray into their fields and Michaels' sheep learned to jump over the highest fences like kangaroos. Jeremy fondly remembered one particular broody hen that was used to sit on ducks' eggs, as the farm's Aylesbury ducks invariably abandoned their nests. The silly hen would anxiously wade after her clutch of ducklings as soon they discovered the pond and began to swim, clucking in alarm after them until the water rose around her neck.

Crazy horses apart, our valley was entirely unspoilt, having never been under the plough or cultivated in any way. Unlike much of South Devon, where the age-old hedges of a dozen small pastures were regularly flattened to provide a soulless corn prairie, these fields had not been touched by pesticides, fertilisers or chemicals of any sort; hence the flora and fauna flourished within nature's immaculate balance. On still summer nights we would wander through the fields towards the river to see the ethereal lights of glow worms in the grass, I have never seen them before or since. We listened to the haunting calls of owls from the oak trees, to curlews and oystercatchers from the estuary and often disturbed a badger or fox out on a hunting trip. The stream that ran down through the valley was overhung with wild honeysuckle, its sweet scent at dusk attracting gigantic Elephant Hawk Moths, their downy wings a tapestry of soft pink and green. One early morning in spring we watched enchanted from our bedroom as a pair of sparring hares had a boxing match on the lawn just four feet from the window. The previous night we had heard strange noises and had gone outside to investigate; perched side by side on the telegraph wire above the garden were five little fluffy shapes, chirruping and hiccupping to each other; as our eyes accustomed themselves to the twilight we could see they were baby barn owls.

But for sheer cuteness some of the tiniest inhabitants of our very un-manicured garden were not easily beaten. I had been sitting on the lawn in the sun one afternoon in early summer when a movement in the grass caught my attention. Within a foot of me appeared a tiny, rotund furry shape that I easily recognised as a bank vole. I watched fascinated and charmed as this enchanting little creature sat quietly warming himself in the sun. Then another appeared and sat close beside the first. A few seconds later a third, fourth and fifth member of this Lilliputian family followed from the bank to join the line up. I sat very still watching them and saw they were definitely sunbathing, like old age pensioners on deck chairs at the seaside. One by one they nodded off, slowly toppling over like skittles and lying fast asleep with their tiny eyes closed! They didn't even wake up when I quietly summoned Jeremy to come and see them; after ten minutes or so the piercing cry of a passing buzzard alerted them and they scuttled off back to the safety of their home in the bank.

Over the years our near neighbour Tony Soper, the famous

broadcaster and naturalist, had often inquired about the valley. No wonder Tony had been so interested in acquiring this exceptionally diverse land, but Michael had resisted his approaches, probably to avoid having to make any kind of decision. In the early autumn our top field sprouted hundreds of enormous velvety field mushrooms; a single one of them fried in butter was as much as you could eat for breakfast. Like my father, I have always delighted in picking and foraging for anything, so we would go armed with plastic bags and usually returned with six bags each after twenty minutes. One September I held a dinner party for which everything on the menu included our mushrooms; the nibbles with drinks were stuffed tiny mushrooms, the starter was marinated mushrooms, followed by main course a mushroom risotto, the evening rounded off with a pudding of mushroom and sherry sorbet. (Not really, though stranger things have been concocted in my kitchen). I gave bags of mushrooms to my parents and friends and froze enough to last until Christmas, by which time we never wanted to see another mushroom.

(Many years later Jeremy and I caught the asparagus festival in Alsace during one of our dozens of overland journeys to Corfu. We had looked forward to it enormously but were bitterly disappointed to discover every single menu featured the short, very fat and unappetisingly white spears, which tasted nothing like the freshly picked green variety we were used to in Devon. The Germans crossed the Rhine again and descended on this festival in their droves; they favoured these stubby spears above all else, probably because they exactly matched their highly prized white Bavarian *weisswurst* sausages. We decided both of these anaemic, unattractive delicacies could do with a couple of hours on a very hot barbecue.)

In late summer blackberries were rampant and I made black-berry jam, bramble mousse and Jeremy's favourite blackberry and apple crumble. In September the wild crab apple trees in the hedges were laden with their tiny red fruits looking like Christmas baubles; Liz gave me her recipe for Crab Apple Jelly and I loved making this, seeing the full jam jars cooling in the kitchen was so satisfying. I must have been a squirrel in a former life. When the snow came, as it regularly did every winter in those days, it transformed the valley into Narnia and Rory had hours of fun sledging down the steeper sloping fields and build-ing snowmen on the lawn in front of the house. The wonderful Raymond Brigg's book *The Snowman* was made into an animated film in 1982, the year Rory was born. I had put the video, along with the book, in his first Christmas stocking and he watched it over and over each year. I think he really believed his snow-man would suddenly come to life and swoop him up into the air.

Our new house was spacious, elegant and comfortable in every season; only very gradually and reluctantly could we come to terms with the idea of selling it before Rory started at prep school. The daily journey would be much too far for him to make as a day boy and we certainly did not want him to board at the age of seven. (Jeremy, like so many unfortunates who were sent away at the age of six, developed many idiosyncrasies as a result and has never been quite the same since. For years after we were married he still shoved his dirty clothes under the bed, well away from Matron's beady eye and the headmaster's cane that would inevitably follow. Years later Miranda and I solved this problem by tossing his accumulated piles of muddy clothes out of the bedroom window, where they were eagerly retrieved from the lawns by our King Charles Cavaliers and dragged away with glee to be nested on in their basket).

If we wanted to take a sabbatical and live overseas again, now would be the time to do it – well before Rory started his serious education. A couple of months before Miranda's arrival was due we took the decision to sell our beautiful home and move to Spain for a couple of years. It had been my suggestion to live near Jávea on the Costa Blanca, where I had spent ten delightful weeks of the spring term at the villa belonging to the owners of my art and finishing school when I was seventeen. Studying a map of the area, Jeremy soon located a new marina under construction at Moraira and within a week he had bought a mooring; it would be a sound investment even if our plans changed and Jeremy certainly wasn't going anywhere without a boat of some description in the frame. In fact neither of us would ever have considered living beside the warm waters of the Mediterranean without a boat, and the search for something suitable for our young family was soon fruitful.

Meanwhile, slightly apprehensive at the thought of moving into a new home in an unfamiliar country with a five-year-old and a baby, I advertised for a suitable nanny and mother's help to accompany us. Two girls made the shortlist and we interviewed both of them at home. The first to arrive was nineteen, attractive and giggly. I didn't take to her. She was far more focused on the idea of coming with us to Spain rather than on the children and never gave Rory as much as a sideways glance. Her goose was well and truly cooked when Jeremy mentioned we would be basing our boat in Spain. She giggled coquettishly and put her hand on my husband's thigh.

"Ooh, I just love boats!" she crooned.

When Rory was four he started in the reception class at a private primary school in Kingsbridge. He looked so angelic in his first green and grey school uniform, complete with smart blazer and cap, but appearances can be deceptive; he was just as mischievous as ever and within the first two days I was summoned by the headmistress who, it was widely known, had little time for boys. In all seriousness she told me Rory had been firing paper pellets at the girls in front of him during maths lessons; no amount of scolding deterred him so she had put him at the back of the classroom where he could play with the toy trucks and cars – a perfect result as far as Rory was concerned. What a terrific grasp of child psychology! Any doubts about the expense of a proper prep school evaporated immediately.

The next girl was eighteen, shy and polite, with a striking resemblance to a young Lady Diana Spencer. Rory grinned over his shoulder at me as he took her hand and led her towards to his bedroom, where I soon heard them chatting and laughing together. Lucinda had completed a two year full time nannying course at a local technical college and seemed competent, if not overly confident. We asked her to begin work a month before Miranda was due, so she could get to know us all before having a new baby to look after. Lucinda moved in with us and was an absolute hit with Rory, making up all sorts of interesting games and educational activities, as well as romping around the garden playing pirates and so on. This was going to be perfect, we thought, and we looked forward to taking her to Spain, where she would surely be such a help with an active little boy.

Miranda was born in the third week of September and the following day we brought her home from hospital to a very thrilled

Rory and Lucinda, who together had decorated the kitchen with pink bunting announcing *Welcome Miranda!* After a cup of tea whilst feeding Miranda, I asked Lucinda to take her to the nursery, change her and give her some boiled water from a bottle. I was feeding Miranda myself but wanted her to get accustomed to a bottle for times when I might have to leave her with Lucinda. I was preparing Rory's early supper when I heard the most fearful scream from Miranda. I ran to the nursery to find Lucinda distraught, holding a scarlet faced baby girl who was howling for all she was worth.

Instinctively I picked up the bottle on the table next to Miranda's cot. It was too hot to hold. Lucinda had tried to give Miranda *boiling* water instead of *cooled*, boiled water. I was livid. How had this girl ever passed her NNEB exams? Of course she was desperately upset but poor Miranda had a scalded mouth and, although only two days old, she would never again take a bottle. After much reflection we decided to give Lucinda a second chance, but from that moment on I let her devote most of her time to keeping Rory amused.

In November Miranda was christened at the church in the nearby village of West Alvington, just as Rory had been five years earlier. As Rory had done, Miranda wore the ivory pure silk christening robe that my grandmother had made for my father in 1919. It had been worn by all the family babies, including my brother Christopher, my cousins and me, ever since; before Rory's christening I had bought some cream silk thread and on the hemline I embroidered tiny initials of all the babies who had worn it. For my outfit I had chosen a long ivory cashmere coat with a high collar and a matching pillbox hat, which I thought very elegant for a winter christening. Our dear lifelong friend

Tony, a talented professional photographer who had taken our wedding pictures, took the photographs. My favourite showed me holding Miranda in the churchyard, with the damp, dark granite church behind me, surrounded by gravestones – very dramatic and atmospheric. The day was bitterly cold, with a threatening, leaden sky; Tony said the photo made me look like a ghostly apparition, which was slightly more flattering than Jeremy's more recent comment that it looked like a publicity shot from *The Addams Family*.

A few weeks beforehand, while Lucinda kept Rory amused, I had made a christening cake using Mummy's Christmas cake recipe, which was always moist and delicious. I had regularly added brandy to the circular fruit cake and waited until the night before the christening to decorate it. I made royal icing coloured to the shade of pale gold straw, then I pressed it down with the crown of my own school straw boater; the result was most effective. I made a flat 'straw' brim around the bottom and tied a wide baby pink satin ribbon around the cake, finishing with a large bow and trailing tails at the back. On the top I used a piping bag to write Miranda's name and the date of her birth in white icing. Exhausted, I eventually finished it at midnight. Lucinda came in to the kitchen first thing next morning to see the cake and asked me why I had written *October* instead of *September* ... Panic! I had obviously suffered a 'new mum' moment. I quickly scraped it off and corrected my crazy mistake. Sadly, the cake was very dry when cut, so I have never made another fruit cake since – that's one less thing as far as I'm concerned.

(Okay I might have got the wrong month, but at least her name was correct. When Miranda was three we decided she was old enough to come with us on a skiing holiday, but Jeremy became momentarily lobotomised when the travel agent asked for the list of his family's names to put on the tickets. All was fine until it came to his daughter's name.

"Ah, yes she's called ... er ... I can see her running around on the lawn ... I've already given you her date of birth, haven't I ... she's three now ... wonderful blonde curls ... JANI! For God's sake, what's her name?"

"What is *who's* name?"

"Our daughter's!"

To be fair we always used her nickname when she was little. I won't embarrass Miranda with it here, but it had obviously supplanted her Christian name in Jeremy's head.)

It was very fortunate that we were employing a nanny during this time, as I was asked to produce and direct a fashion show for an exclusive boutique in Kingsbridge, the owner and her husband being old friends who had been amongst our guests at the fateful house warming party and also at Miranda's christening. The show was to be held at the Thurlestone Hotel, which had been owned by our friends' family for many years. Penny had two young daughters and was only too happy for me to bring Miranda in her pram to all the meetings and models' fittings in the boutique, so I could feed her when necessary. The show was in aid of the RNLI and I asked our Salcombe station if they could provide a couple of lifeboatmen to open the show. I was thrilled when they agreed and I arranged for the opening scene to have a film projected onto the back of the stage showing a lifeboat plunging into rough seas, with the models forming a tableau in raincoats; the two hairy lifeboatmen in full kit, complete with life jackets and sou'westers, stood on either side. The music was *A Life on the Ocean Wave* played by the band of the Royal Marines and as the curtains parted there was an effusive round of applause from the audience, many of whom were stalwart ladies who regularly rattled the RNLI collecting boxes in the towns and villages of the South Hams. Jeremy and Lucinda brought Rory and Miranda to the evening show, where the press photographer took a sweet colour photo of Rory, Miranda and me for the local paper.

It was less fortunate when Rory contracted chickenpox a month after Miranda was born. Lucinda, lacking immunity, promptly returned to her family, so I suddenly found myself alone with one very poorly child and a babe in arms. I am immune to the usual childhood diseases, having been thrown into bed with one or other of my young cousins whenever they contracted any illness; thankfully Miranda developed just one tiny spot on her hairline, having inherited my immunity. Twice a day I delicately painted Rory's spots with calamine lotion to soothe the bothersome itching, counting them at his insistence; he had 185, poor child. Fortunately my parents came to help, as this was precisely the week at the beginning of November that Jeremy had decided to deliver our new boat to Spain. He had meticulously planned the arduous journey to ensure he would be back in time to be present at Miranda's christening, which of course he was not.

Chapter 3 – Jeremy
Chickenpox and the Thief of Biscay

Once the travel bug bites there is no known antidote, and I know that I shall be happily infected until the end of my life.

Michael Palin

Though it had seemed a great deal longer to me, one and a half years had flashed by since the ashes of our former home had been bulldozed into the earth; but at last the new house was ready enough for my family to occupy. Most of the rooms awaited their second coats of paint and the gardens would take much longer to tame, but once more we had a home of our own. Over the following months the finer details of the house were gradually completed as finances allowed; even the gardens began to look established. Broad meandering paths from the house were mown though the meadows to the old quay by our ruined lime kiln; ponies for Rory came and went, and sheep were brought in to graze the rest of the wild pasture. Looking around at what we had achieved it occurred to us that we were now the owners of a very desirable property, one that had cost us little beyond raw materials and many thousands of hours of our own relentless toil in all weathers.

Glorious as it was, we knew life in our new home could not last forever. For it had also dawned on us that Rory would be starting at prep school as soon as he was seven; the only two worthwhile contenders in the area were over twenty miles distant, but neither Jani nor I intended to send him away to board at that tender age. My own experience of boarding from the age of six at my first prep school had been an unspeakable horror of sadism, and worse, that I could not risk inflicting on my son. My mother had eventually seen the light and after four terms of misery I was moved to a much happier place; but of course there was no counselling in those days, no delving into the issues of one's empowerment, self-internalisation, wellbeing or general mental health with its long menu of neat pigeonhole acronyms. One simply got on with it.

More practically neither Jani nor I could face the idea of driving for five hours – and six in the summer – every day during term time. There were no school coaches in those days and no other parents in the area with whom to share the burden; use of the local bus service would involve our young son leaving home at six in the morning to return at eight in the evening.

Faced with such a dilemma, and however painful the decision might be, there was no escaping the unpalatable truth: at some point we would have to move within striking range of Rory's prep school. Not for the first time in our lives my father thought us barking mad to consider such an idea – selling one's house and moving purely for the benefit of one's children was absolutely not on one's agenda, as indeed he had never allowed such a sacrifice to cross my mother's mind. In the eventuality Jani and I would move house twice more for the benefit of our children's schooling during the following ten years.

(When at the age of eleven my own entry to public school loomed large, I had been determined to opt for an institution that was reasonably close to home; at least I might stand a chance of getting home at half-term. During an interview at an esteemed school situated a full four counties away from Devon, the brutish headmaster – attired to impart maximum terror in black gown and mortarboard – asked me for my current position in class. Instantly I spotted an opportunity to queer my own pitch: without hesitation I facetiously replied that I usually sat in the third row, second from the left. The ogre roared at me, singularly unimpressed by my impudence and probably would have given me a good whacking there and then, had my mother not been waiting outside to drive me back to prep school. How different our experience had been at Millfield thirty-five years later when Rory's turn came. At the end of a heartening meeting with the headmaster, a most inspiring man, Christopher Martin shook hands with young Rory and left him with the parting words 'May fortune smile upon you'. Perhaps he always signed off with such a farewell – in fact we knew he did not – but it wouldn't have mattered if it was so; the truth was that the headmaster had the perspicacity to recognise a boy who would benefit from a small kindness after a somewhat daunting day. Our decision to choose Millfield, taken with Rory, had been made in that moment).

As the prospect of our self-enforced move drew closer, the tantalising chance to take a sabbatical abroad before Rory's education began in earnest was beginning to look tempting. Besides, the fire had caused us to reassess the direction of our lives; we were far from well off by most people's standards, but I was fortunate enough to be able to manage my meagre investments from the end of any telephone line. The relative security of our position had hitherto allowed me to imagine I could plan my life many years ahead without the slightest care. Then came the rude reminder of life's fragility, so recently highlighted by our escape from the fire, which had abruptly brought the far horizons into sharper focus. At some point while age and health were still on our side, I pondered, we should cease the constant quest for more and settle for what we were fortunate enough to have, even if school fees would remain a continuous struggle. So once again we were obstinately determined to exchange tepid and mild for ice and fire, monochrome for colour, predictability for serendipity and existence for life – life to be grabbed by the scruff of the neck and vigorously shaken.

We had thoroughly enjoyed and lavished love on our new home for less than three and a half years when we decided to bite the bullet and put it up for sale. The first advertisement in Country Life attracted plenty of interest and after the usual shakedown there remained two very keen bidders. Our beautiful valley was a virgin flower meadow, home to several species of rare butterfly, untouched by chemicals of any description; within living memory it had never been cultivated. Its acres were home to every form of native wildlife; its private foreshore even provided nesting places for swans and ducks; its hedges, covers and spinneys were home to badger and fox, hare and rabbit, pheasant and partridge, owl and buzzard, stoat and weasel alike. So who would be the very last person we would want to continue our careful stewardship of this land? Certainly not the owner of a national fertilizer and agri-chemical business, but it was he who had made the best offer. Our scruples had to be set aside if we were going to achieve the best price, particularly as a slice of the proceeds would be going towards our children's education.

Our preferred buyers were a delightful couple in their fifties who were keen ornithologists and committed conservationists. The home they had recently sold was a fabulous house set in the middle of its own island on the River Thames, which had become a renowned haven for waterfowl during their caring watch. I telephoned them after we had received the excellent but unwanted offer from our industrialist bidder, explaining that we would so very much prefer them to take over the reins of our special property. We had a deadline to accept the existing offer and I asked if they could match the bid before it was too late. Alas, their letter formally offering an even higher figure arrived twelve hours after the agreed deadline had passed. I didn't know whether to laugh or cry when I noticed the second-class stamp on the envelope, knowing the ancient biodiversity of our valley would soon be ploughed up, denuded of its pretty hedges and manicured into a genteel, faux parkland. And all for the sake of one first class stamp.

Completion date for the sale our home had been set for the middle of December. Our new destination was a circle on the map of eastern Spain centred on the Marina Alta region, for which Jani nursed fond memories of several blossom scented months spent with the eccentric lady who based her finishing school in Jávea for the Spring term. There had been other considerations of course, such as suitable primary schooling for Rory, but in truth ours had been a lame, apron-strings sort of choice. Spain after all was a stable, fairly civilized country that was conveniently close and easily accessible, as well as calling itself home to many British citizens – several hundred thousand too many, some might have said.

Our horizon had appeared boundless at the time; we could equally have considered some extraordinary properties that were out of favour and going for a song, but each of them had their own catalogue of drawbacks. Jani discounted an absurdly romantic twenty bedroom chateau set amidst the pine forests of Aquitaine at the prospect of fearsome spiders, scorpions and poisonous caterpillars, while a modernist boathouse on the south shore of Sydney Harbour was dismissed at the thought of shark infested water at the bottom of its garden and even more enormous and venomous spiders. The temptation of a laird's sporting estate deep in the Scottish Highlands was somewhat harder to resist; it was vast and imposing, having a mile-long drive displaying a warning sign at its gates stating that cars should give way to aircraft. But eventually we decided such a pile would be untenable without a private helicopter to access the place, one's own oil company to heat it, an aerial crop spraying enterprise to annihilate the midges, and an innate sense of direction to navigate from one end of the castle to the other. There were several less extravagant options too, but on this occasion our delusions of grandeur had been reined in by a bout of uncharacteristic circumspection and frugality.

Accordingly my family were set on a two year break in Spain, although with the gift of hindsight I wish Jani had twisted my arm far harder to give Corfu another chance; the island so lovingly and enigmatically described by Gerald Durrell would have been her first choice by a long way. Conversely my own impression of Corfu, gained after my one and only visit in the mid 1970s, had been consigned to the same locker as indelible memories of mumps and the rubbery smell of the dentist's gas mask. A girlfriend had jilted me just hours before the outset of a romantic week in the Ionian, which had been most eagerly anticipated on my part; loath to waste both tickets I had flown out alone with a well thumbed copy of *Prospero's Cell* in a glum, introspective mood matched only by the island's wettest October in decades.

The dirt roads to my soulless concrete hotel had mostly been washed away, leaving me and my few fellow guests stranded and isolated until a coach struggled through to return us to the airport a week later. My recollection of those seven interminable, storm lashed days and nights on a desolate stretch of the island's west coast at the fag-end of the season, largely spent at a soggy beach bar in the company of the only other guest within a tortoise's lifespan of my own age – Raymond, a lugubrious tripe butcher from Bridgwater – should never have held such sway. Now, as I look back on my family's fifteen year love affair with Corfu, which blossomed a decade after we had returned after our Spanish sabbatical, I find I shall never be able to forgive myself. And for so very many reasons.

Jani and I sorely missed our carefree years in Cyprus, yet we hoped Spain would manage to replicate at least some of the peculiarly chaotic, endearingly anarchic delights of life amongst the Cypriots. Spain offered us two very different but equally beguiling alternatives: a serene life in the countryside, well away from the crowded coasts, or a more adventurous life afloat; ideally we wanted to enjoy the stimulating contrasts of both options. We had been landlubbers for five long years since returning from Cyprus and quickly decided a modest boat and a small house inland would provide a safer and more prudent investment. After all we intended to live in Spain for less than two years, so readily saleable assets that stood some chance of turning a profit were essential. But Jani was expecting our second child to be born in September and that imminent event would necessarily affect our choice of boat. A traditional sailing boat, with a glorified ladder providing access to its accommodation, was out of the question with a babe in arms; equally another catamaran was ruled out on the grounds of expense, as we would need something substantially larger than our beloved Aries for the four of us and our guests to occupy in any comfort.

There had only been one recurring bone of contention during our honeymoon voyage to Cyprus, namely Jani's inability to dry and straighten her waist length hair properly during the many days and nights we were at sea. Ever keen to placate my new bride before we left English shores, and all too familiar with her dread of curly hair, I had dutifully bought the largest portable generator that could be fitted into the sail locker beneath Aries' foredeck. Believing I could simply winch the heavy brute from its stowage and start it up whenever mains electricity was required for hair drying purposes, I considered the problem well and truly solved. I should have known better.

The first occasion our new generator had been used in anger came moments after our anchor had hit the seabed in front of the La Coruña Yacht Club in Northern Spain. We had been at sea for four days and nights across Biscay and I was decidedly tired after standing most of the night watches; but Jani was chomping at the bit to go shopping for some postcards and delicious fresh produce ashore, for which perfectly dried and straightened hair would be an absolute necessity. She was after all, still a fashion model at the time and would never have dreamt of going anywhere without looking her best, whether in jeans or evening dress. So out came the generator, accompanied by a good deal of heaving, cursing and bruising in the July heat.

I had been expecting Jani to appear from our cabin with a neat little hairdryer of the pink plastic variety; instead she emerged wielding something the size of an industrial leaf blower that looked more suitable for melting residual pig iron from the inside of a blast furnace. (If I had inspected this beast more carefully before we left England I would already have known that the National Grid had to fire up the Drax B power station whenever Jani switched it on.) Inevitably my spanking new generator expired in a shower of sparks as soon as Jani attempted to straighten her hair with the monster dryer. Thenceforward, and here was the rub, she had to put up with frizzy hair for the next five weeks of our voyage to Cyprus. To be fair Jani hardly complained at all about her many bad hair days – well, not when she was asleep.

Following my abject failure to buy a powerful enough generator to run her 'very modest' hairdryer, Jani found the perfect solution in Minorca. She bought twenty outsize, vivid pink plastic hair rollers with the intention of letting her hair dry in the hot sun. The first time my wife appeared, like Shirley Temple on steroids, wearing a headful of these as we prepared to take a tour of Mahon's historic harbour in the dinghy, I flatly refused to be seen with her.

For our own very different reasons this was a fashion disaster neither of us had ever forgotten. With this and more practical considerations in mind we decided a motor boat might be a more suitable answer for the next two years of our lives. Reluctantly I held my nose and began the search for a likely craft with a strong hull and all mod cons, including air conditioning, central heating and an extremely powerful generator. Unfortunately I couldn't find anything within my self-imposed budget in Spain, or even in the Western Mediterranean. Instead I located the ideal boat in Jersey, a powerful forty-foot model of the rakish chrome and smoked glass variety. When Jani first caught sight of *Seahawk*, with its low aquiline bow rising to a high superstructure further astern, she declared with justification that it looked like a floating steam iron. However Seahawk was in pristine condition, having spent most of its very short life cossetted in St Helier marina as a floating display platform for champagne buckets and extravagant vases of gladioli.

More gin gazebo than gin palace, it (certainly not a *she*) boasted two sumptuous double cabins and a crew cabin, a pair of chintzy ensuite bathrooms, a well appointed galley, a large flying bridge and – most importantly for us – a spacious, well shaded and high sided cockpit that would be ideal for a young child and a baby. Sliding patio doors connected the cockpit seamlessly to the saloon, where aquamarine Wilton carpets, yards of mock suede trim, plush velvet covered sofas, a mahogany dining table and a truly vulgar, mirror-clad cocktail bar awaited. All in all it was well designed for swanky marina life, if far less so for putting to sea in the English Channel – let alone the Bay of Biscay. One visiting friend, famous for his many Malapropisms, had remarked that the lavish interior must have been designed by Burt Bacharach. I had been about to suggest he probably meant Jon Bannenberg, the famous superyacht designer, but on reflection I had to agree with him: Seahawk's interior décor really was excessively Burt Bacharach.

Our dear little Miranda arrived on 18th September without a hitch for mother and baby, although I had complained loudly about the exceedingly uncomfortable armchair I was given during the overnight labour process. Jani's private room, I protested, had cost a small fortune and I had expected my own couchette, room service and a minibar at the very least. My re-monstrations did not go down at all well, even if my gripes had in truth been intended to distract my long suffering wife from her contractions. Our separate recollections of that long night are still wildly at odds, but Jani did receive *some* foot massages, even if the iced flannels never made an appearance – ice and hospital canteens being incompatible.

As soon as Jani and baby Miranda were fully settled at home with my in-laws a few days later, I flew over to Jersey to bring Seahawk back to Devon. I had originally planned to take it to Spain the following Spring, but impatience and a sudden thirst for adventure persuaded me to deliver the boat at the beginning of November as soon as I had checked all the boat's systems to my own satisfaction. This was definitely not a trip for the faint-hearted; in fact I don't believe anyone has been stupid enough to attempt the trip directly across the Bay of Biscay in such a vessel at any time of year – let alone in stormy November. Thirty-eight, it turns out, is not too young to be beset by early-onset midlife crisis, however rare the affliction may be at such a tender age; for once, at least, I could claim that I was exceptionally advanced for my years.

Early in the morning of 1st November Seahawk was ready to cast off from her temporary berth at Torquay Marina. John, an experienced sailing friend, had kindly offered to come along for the trip; my other crew was an apprentice marine engineer who was keen to put some ocean miles on his qualification 'ticket'. I didn't know young Jason at all, but I soon realised I should have obtained further references when he showed up bleary-eyed seven hours after our planned departure time – a delay that threw all my calculations into confusion. The weather could not have been more perfect for the first leg of our delivery across the channel to Camaret-sur-Mer, a charming little fishing port south of Brest in Brittany, but we arrived too late in the evening to buy fuel. The intention had been to refuel Seahawk at Camaret and press on over Biscay through the night before the weather closed in again. So much for that idea.

Sure enough the narrow window of fair weather slammed shut and we became stormbound for five days in Camaret, a period that was exactly long enough for the three of us to sample the entire menu and wine list of the only restaurant open out of season. That was no great hardship and after our second evening we were welcomed like old friends; generous glasses of *Fine de Bretagne*, the local variety of Calvados, were invariably pressed upon us before we returned aboard in disorderly fashion. The morning trip ashore for fresh croissants and dishes of delicious French coffee was followed by a trudge along the coast to clear our heads until we reached the Point de Penhir. Thence we could gaze in awe from beneath our hoods at the distant turmoil of the Raz de Sein, the infamously treacherous tide race through which Seahawk would eventually have to battle on its course into the Bay of Biscay.

As the sixth morning dawned over Camaret a small gap in the procession of Atlantic depressions gave us the chance to set off; the first fifteen hours of the trip would be demandingly rough, but at least the wind and seas would be behind us and were forecast to abate considerably when we approached the north-westernmost tip of Spain. For the next twenty hours we hurtled across Biscay, harnessed in turn to the helmsman's seat while delicately adjusting the throttles and wheel as the boat fought its way over each crest and through each trough. As the miles mounted up I began to fully appreciate the enormity of this undertaking; the red glow of the instruments and the loom of our navigation lights in the driven spume only emphasised our insignificance amidst the infinite darkness in a boat that suddenly felt no bigger than a skiff on the Serpentine.

As foretold the seas gradually abated before dawn the following morning and we made a comfortable approach to Bayona on the north-western coast of Spain, where we arrived battered, badly bruised and thoroughly exhausted from our rodeo ride across five-hundred miles of rough seas. I was grateful we hadn't been sunk by a half-submerged shipping container or tree trunk as Seahawk sped blindly through the night, but that relief turned to horror if ever I shudderingly imagined the consequences of such a collision in those lonely seas. Two days later we tied up in Gibraltar after a taxing passage around Cape St Vincent, thoroughly relieved the worst was over. Now there only remained the more benign Mediterranean sea between us and Seahawk's new home near Jávea; that passage would surely be most agreeable after the punishment we had taken in the Atlantic.

Only then, as I shaved before going ashore that morning, did I notice the livid rash of spots on my face; closer inspection revealed many more eruptions all over my body. I was suddenly feeling distinctly under the weather, having had a vague suspicion – quickly dismissed at the time – that I had been running a temperature from the moment we left Bayona. Jason, our thoroughly indolent third crew member was still in bed, so John and I wandered over to the marina office to stretch our legs and arrange for a diesel delivery. A call to Jani from a telephone kiosk confirmed my worst suspicions: back in Devon poor Rory was pickled with chickenpox and I was certain to follow. John and I allowed ourselves a slap-up breakfast before ambling despondently back to Seahawk, knowing that our leisurely night's rest in Gibraltar had gone by the board; now we needed to complete

Seahawk's delivery before I became properly ill.

If I had been furious to discover that Jason had jumped ship during my brief absence ashore, absconding with all the cash from the desk in my cabin, I was calling for bloody retribution when John informed me his wallet had also been emptied. Why had I been cursed with such a trusting nature? John and I hot-footed straight to the Police Station near the commercial port, where an extremely helpful detective quickly ascertained that Jason had boarded a flight to London not ten minutes earlier; the plane had already taken off, but our detective wasn't prepared to give up our cause without a fight. Undeterred, he suggested young Jason might perhaps have used the considerable sum of stolen cash to buy drugs, or maybe even a gun. John and I sat on our hands like dunces, entirely unreceptive to the policeman's blatant prompting despite his quizzically raised eyebrow. Better still, the detective continued with a blatantly exaggerated wink, could it be implied that our mechanic had nursed some fascination with Irish terrorists?

Catching his drift at last John and I concurred effusively, whereupon the patient man immediately put in a call to his colleagues at Heathrow airport. There, two hours later, our good-for-nothing crewman was subjected to an embarrassingly thorough body search involving large men and rubber gloves, whereupon he was relieved of his ill-gotten cash – most of which was eventually returned to us fully washed, disinfected and ironed. Vengeance on this occasion was sweet indeed, but ironically our efficient detective's references to terrorism would soon return to haunt him. Only a few months later he starred as a key witness at the official inquiry into 'Operation Flavius', the shooting of three IRA personnel at the hands of the British SAS in Gibraltar.

Feeling unduly pleased with ourselves John and I set Seahawk's course into the Mediterranean and along the coast of Andalusia, already aware that our delay with the police had ruined any chances of reaching our final destination the same day. Nightfall found Seahawk near Cartagena, lying a few hundred yards off the coast as we prepared to enter the tiny harbour at Mazarron, where we could conveniently catch a few hours sleep before the final dash up the coast to Moraira. The harbour entrance was littered with islets and shallows that were utterly invisible in the blackness, all of which made our approach quite tricky. John and I were sitting at the helm on the flying bridge, studying the radar screen and drawing compass bearings on the chart, when a dazzling searchlight lit us up like a fairground. A loudhailer echoed across the sea and a stern voice ordered us to stop our engines and prepare to be searched. Against the glare we could just discern the outline of a very large and rather aged coastguard cutter, which had managed to creep up on us unseen in the starless night. Evidently the sight of Seahawk powering along the coast in the middle of a bleak November night had raised some suspicion in an area popular with drug runners.

The cutter's deck lights flickered into life and we were able to observe the farce enfolding before us, as a boarding party prepared to launch their rigid inflatable over the side from a derrick amidships. Unfortunately the ungainly old tub was rolling like a barrel in the heavy swell and, as the inflatable was raised from its chocks with the crew of five already strapped into their seats, it began to swing dangerously over the ship's deck like a wrecking ball. After several increasingly life threatening swoops over the deck the winch operator decided to panic. At the limit of one crazy arc through the air the little boat was unceremoniously let go, whereupon it plunged a full ten feet and hit the sea below with a report like a gunshot. The occupants must have been badly winded by the fall, but after a much tugging at the outboard motor's starter cord, their craft came racing over the waves towards us. Moments later the balaclava-clad crew were alongside us. The man in the bows climbed nimbly into our cockpit and his portly commanding officer prepared to follow just as a particularly heavy swell swept past, plunging him ignominiously into the sea between the two boats. Balaclavas alone could not hide the crew's mirth as the wretched officer splashed about furiously in search of his beret. John and I eventually managed to grab a braided epaulette each and hauled the gasping fellow into our cockpit, where he floundered like a hooked cod at the feet of his sniggering crew. Ignoring the muzzles of their pistols, I slid open one of the saloon doors and returned moments later with some towels and a generous glass of whisky, which the shivering officer gratefully downed. It was safe to say I now had the upper hand.

The youngest amongst the boarding party spoke excellent English, and it was to him I explained why I was on passage at such an inhospitable time of year, adding as I pointed to my spotty face that I was succumbing to chickenpox. The *Commandante* accepted our translated excuses and hastily called off the search at the first mention of *la varicela*; however he did ask if there was any more whisky to be had. After a cursory inspection of the saloon the boarding party went on their way, having 'confiscated' the bottle of single malt I had just opened. Fortunately they never found the wholesale quantities of Johnson's baby powder Jani had stowed in the crew cabin amongst the boxes of Pampers nappies. White powder in plastic bags might have required a somewhat lengthier explanation.

Next morning I eased Seahawk onto its new marina berth at Moraira; but with a rising fever and a face resembling the bubbly surface of a raspberry blancmange I was in no mood for celebration. Bidding farewell to John as he left for the airport, I headed blearily to a letting agent in search of a furnished villa for us to rent until we found a suitable house to buy. A fairly large villa was called for as Jani's parents and our nanny would be with us for Christmas; Seahawk was of course too small to accommodate all seven of us in any comfort. Eventually I was taken to view an inoffensive house above Moraira, standing in a private plot amongst dozens of identical villas. It had more than enough bedrooms and was well enough presented in the contrived holiday villa style. Although it was modern and reasonably well built by local standards, it felt desperately cold and damp inside, all the shutters having been closed against the sun since the end of the summer. Before signing the contract I asked the agent to ensure the oil tank was filled, that the heating was turned on and the house was fully aired in good time for my family's scheduled arrival a week before Christmas.

Mission accomplished I wandered back to the marina and gratefully took to my cabin, where I could rue the folly of Seahawk's costly delivery at leisure: I had been robbed by a trusted crew member who had almost put the entire trip in jeopardy from the outset, one very expensive bottle of fifteen year-old whisky had been confiscated and 10,000 litres of diesel had been guzzled by Seahawk's thirsty engines during the trip. But extraordinarily our gin gazebo had acquitted itself well, completing the 1600 mile delivery from South Devon without damage to its hull or serious injury to its crew, all of which was surely against the odds.

Seahawk could now revert to type, to its former life of

indolence in which it would only poke its nose out of the marina for appearance's sake. The eastern seaboard of the Spain thereabouts was bereft of anchorages sheltered from the uncomfortable swells rolling incessantly up or down the coast; if you wanted to go for a day's jaunt you turned either left or right out of Moraira and headed for the next gabion-enclosed marina, which was not our idea of fun. Seahawk would only come into its own during the summer trips we had already planned to the more hospitable Balearic Islands, where shelter around their indented coasts could always be found in calm anchorages. In the meantime the boat would serve as a comfortable weekend caravan, a novelty for friends to visit for lunch around the cockpit table, no different to the rest of its ostentatious cousins. Seahawk was never going to be a boat to win our affections, I reflected, even though it had been carefully chosen for its purpose.

Much later that night, and to my eternal shame, I buttoned my sailing jacket tight under my chin and took a taxi to Alicante airport and boarded a flight to Gatwick at the very height of my infectiousness. I had carefully swaddled myself in scarf, woolly hat and sunglasses, but my disguise could have done little to hide an angry pebbledash of spots and the telltale glow of a raging fever. I had been unaware that chickenpox could be quite such an unpleasant illness in adults, but I had my daughter's christening to attend and I was determined to return in time. On the early morning train from London I tried in vain to buoy myself up with the words of Peter Cook's *The Ballad of Spotty Muldoon*, until a sallow youth happened to sit down opposite me. Timidly sporting the most luxuriant crop of acne I had ever seen, he gave me a knowing smile of commiseration as I ruefully sank further into my collar. When the poor wretch alighted at the next station he turned to glance back at me again in disbelief, no doubt reassuring himself that his sinecure as Britain's official mascot of maculation had finally been usurped. Four hours later I staggered onto the platform at Totnes, where I fully expected to find Jani waiting for me with oodles of sympathy and calamine lotion.

Chapter 4 – Jani
Y Viva España

All our dreams can come true if we have the courage to pursue them.

Walt Disney.

Jeremy had telephoned from Gatwick soon after his flight had landed, informing me he would be on the early morning train from Paddington and asking if I could meet him at Totnes. It was an agreeably sunny and unseasonably warm lunchtime for November as I parked the car and went into the station. I stood in the middle of the long platform as the London train pulled in and scanned the disembarking passengers for Jeremy, who unaccountably wasn't among them. I sighed in resignation; obviously he had missed the connection from the airport and I would have to drive all the way home and repeat the journey later in the day. As it was a Friday the platform was bustling with people and I suddenly thought I should check that I hadn't missed him in the crowd. Retracing my steps as I passed the passengers making their way to the exit, I heard a pitiful croak behind me calling my name. I turned around to take a second look at the tall thin man in a heavy jacket I had just passed. Hunched over and clasping himself as if in pain, with a woolly hat pulled low over his forehead and a scarf pulled tightly around his neck, the poor wretch's unshaven face was the colour and texture of scarlet porridge. It was my husband. As I hugged him I could feel him shuddering with cold through his layers of clothing, despite the warmth of the day.

"I've had this fever for two days," he croaked, "so I tried to disguise myself before I boarded the plane."

This was the 21st November, I reminded Jeremy, the day before Miranda's christening. We were expecting a houseful of guests and there was still so much to prepare for the party after the church service.

"I think I can still make it if I dose myself up," he said hopefully.

"Absolutely not!" I replied. "You're infectious and you'll pass it on to everyone."

I drove this dejected apparition home and put him to bed with a hot water bottle, a mug of Earl Grey and some paracetamol. The following day he was still running a high temperature, so after feeding Miranda I took him some toast and coffee in bed. Lucinda the nanny had returned and took charge of Rory, dressing him in his sailor suit ready for the short church service, after which the congregation of twenty adults, the vicar and a dozen children came back to the house for tea, christening cake and Champagne. Much later when I popped in to see Jeremy after everyone had left, he meekly asked if he could possibly have some tea and cake too. I had almost forgotten he was there.

Jeremy's illness was most inconvenient. We were due to complete the sale of our home less than three weeks after the christening, before which all our belongings and furniture would have to be packed up and removed. Another few days after that my parents, our nanny, our two young children and I were booked on a flight to Alicante. We sincerely hoped Jeremy would already be there in time to meet us at the airport, having successfully driven out to Spain.

* * *

To explain why the area around Jávea was chosen as our destination I must wind the clock back to 1969.

Our ferry, the *Hispania*, tossed and rolled in the confused seas of the English Channel like a toy boat in a washing machine, having left Southampton that evening in the teeth of a December gale. Extraordinarily I never felt seasick in those days and I found the 36-hour passage a great adventure. At the age of seventeen I was a pupil at a small finishing school in South Devon. The owners of Chantry School of Art, known to its nine pupils as Auntie Vicky and Uncle Peter – and indirectly as AV and UP – had kindly offered to take me with them in their VW Microbus to Spain, where the other girls would be flying out to join us for the Spring term.

After dinner during our second night at sea, somewhere in mid-Biscay, the ship's band bravely struck up in the sedate ballroom of the rather old fashioned ship. AV and UP were both on the stout side and did not venture onto the highly polished ballroom floor, but as it was New Year's Eve they must have felt sorry for me having no partner to dance with. Then just as the ship lurched for the umpteenth time, causing our drinks to skate across the table, a tall young Spaniard slid sideways across the floor in our direction. He stopped in front of me and asked me to dance; I was thrilled, even more so when the band leader announced that there was a dancing competition for anyone brave enough to enter. I danced with my partner to everything the band could offer, as the judge gradually eliminated the other couples. Three athletic young Russian men made valiant efforts to perform the extraordinarily strenuous Cossack dance or Hopak, which must have been impossibly difficult with the ship rolling from side to side; AV and UP surmised that they could have been dancers from the Bolshoi.

Eventually my dancing partner and I were the only couple left and we were awarded our prizes of vouchers to spend in the ship's duty free shop. I was delighted and rushed there first thing the following morning, spending my £5 voucher on a bottle of Yves St. Laurent 'Y' eau de toilette. Whenever I smell that scent it always reminds me of that wild night in the middle of the Bay of Biscay. I think I slept on our pile of luggage in the back of the bus most of the way from Bilbao to Biarritz, where AV was exhibiting some of her paintings in a gallery near the sea front. I wasn't allowed out of the bus as she couldn't trust me not to get carried away in the glamorous shops. Our next stop was in Zaragoza, where we spent the night. After dinner we visited the impressive Baroque *Nuestra Señora del Pilar* Cathedral, which was bathed throughout by the flickering glow of thousands of candles. Utterly beautiful and ethereal. Eventually we arrived in Jávea and climbed halfway up the hill of *Calvario*, where the Microbus finally pulled into the drive of AV's pretty villa. With terraces overlooking acres of orange groves leading to the pueblo, then onwards to the tiny picturesque puerto and shimmering sea beyond, the villa must have been much larger than I remember in order to accommodate all of us girls.

As soon as the other girls arrived in Jávea, life at the villa became awash with fun and laughter; the sun shone every day and our lessons primarily consisted of art, history of art, and Spanish, which were often taught al fresco. The mundane sub-jects of a finishing school, such as flower arranging, ballet, basic *savoir faire* and how to climb out of a sports car with decorum, had already been touched upon during our first term – AV rightly assumed none of us girls were much interested in the more snobbish and obsolescent social graces. Our classes were over by lunchtime, after which AV imaginatively arranged for a local flamenco dancer to give us lessons; other afternoons were filled with pottery classes given by a German lady in the village, and with very basic cookery instruction from AV, who was actually a Cordon Bleu cook. After my first attempt at a Spaghetti Bolognese, when I burnt the mincemeat and ruined one of her precious English saucepans, AV excused me from further culinary instruction and suggested I practice my drawing skills instead. In my report at the end of that term, under the heading 'Cookery', AV wrote *Jani swings between extreme fastidiousness and slap happy muddle*. Nothing much has changed since then. One evening each week we were treated to a performance by a brilliant classical guitarist who played for us in the candlelit sitting room. As romantic young girls, our favourite pieces were the *Romance Anonimo* and the Adagio from Roderigo's *Concierto de Aranjuez*, still as enchantingly haunting today as when I first heard them all those years ago in Jávea. (These can both be enjoyed on YouTube, and one clip shows a guitarist performing at the Jávea Parador).

My fellow pupils had come to Chantry from all corners of the globe. Jenny was from Peru, Liz was an American living in South Africa, Ginetta was Italian, Maggie was Swedish, my room mate Fiona came from a grand house in Kent, Stephi lived in Leicestershire, two of us were from South Devon and Annys came from Cornwall. We were, to put it mildly, a decidedly unusual bunch and it didn't take some of us very long to suspect we had all had been secretly sent to Chantry and thrown together at great expense as part of some rehabilitation and correction program. Five decades later Fi and I still wonder about that.

During that term we had been very fortunate to have AV as our guide to the art galleries of Madrid, Toledo and Valencia. With her photographic memory and quicksilver intellect, she had become fluent in five languages at a young age; later she had been one of the interpreters at the Nuremberg Trials. More importantly for us she was an extraordinarily knowledgeable teacher who could rattle off a donnish lecture on any of the Old Masters from the top of her head; she made every subject fascinating and amusing, often peppering our lectures with anecdotes of her time as a young driver in the ATS during the war. One of her stories in particular chimes with me now, because I have a recurring nightmare exactly like it. She described an evening she was supposed to be off duty; she had just washed her hair when she was suddenly called to drive her colonel to a cocktail party in the officers' mess. She crammed her army cap over her rollers and drove him to the party, whereupon the colonel insisted she joined him; she spent the rest of the evening petrified he would ask her to remove her cap. Her fruity language from those days came as a revelation and we sheltered young things delighted in picking up some choice expressions, much to the horror of our parents.

We spent a few days in each city, invariably staying at yet another Hotel des Anglais, where we girls soon discovered a marvellous invention called Room Service. After each day of traipsing around the galleries until our brains buzzed with all the information AV tried to cram into our heads about every single artist, we would return to the hotel with aching feet and order an enormous afternoon tea. This was wheeled to our rooms on a procession of trolleys and our unhappy parents had these extravagances added to their bills at the end of term; fortunately for them our taste for alcohol hadn't yet developed.

All of us would be taking Art and History of Art 'A' levels during the summer term, but I was also taking my English 'A' level, for which the private tutor from Chantry corresponded with me by air mail. I was the only girl taking English and it became a lonely task to translate Chaucer, or to memorise Shakespeare and my other set books in such distracting surroundings. Set essays were sent by Air Mail to Devon and my tutor, Roland, sent them back marked with comments in red ink. I took it as a personal insult if I received anything less than an 'A' and told Roland how hurt and upset I was, making him feel so guilty that after a few weeks I always got the mark I wanted. As spring came to the Costa Blanca the countryside around us was transformed by a froth of pale pink almond blossom; huge freesias grew wild by the roadsides and the scent of orange and lemon blossom pervaded everything. The oranges we picked from the trees were outsized, sweet and bursting with juice; they were so fresh and crisp that each segment snapped open when you bit into it. I loved Jávea and the surrounding Marina Alta area; Dénia held a fabulous street market every Tuesday and we had great fun looking at all the tempting wares displayed on the dusty pavements while AV did her weekly shopping. She would wait for us at a favourite café in the leafy main street of Dénia, where we would meet for refreshments in the shade of the plane trees before returning to Jávea. Our favourite snacks were bocadillos – crusty baguette style rolls filled with hot slices of tender roast pork and a splash of savoury gravy. In those blissful pre-burger and full English breakfast days, we girls went into the kitchens and taught the cooks how to make chips, which then appeared on their menu soon afterwards. I can only apologise to you all. What had we done!

I didn't drink coffee in those days; instead I opted for hot milk served in a tall glass with the customary packets of sugar in the saucer. One morning I woke to find my whole body pickled with an alarming looking scarlet rash, although I felt perfectly well and it wasn't itchy or painful. However AV was in a flap, shutting me in my bedroom in case I was contagious and calling the local Spanish doctor. He came to the villa to examine me and was at a loss to explain my symptoms until I mentioned I was allergic to penicillin, whereupon he asked if I drank a lot of milk. He beamed as I answered, closed his notebook with a flourish and explained that dairy cows in Spain were regularly (and illegally) given massive doses of penicillin.

Another incident that must surely have given AV palpitations happened within the first week of term. Two uniformed officers from the local Guardia Civil appeared at the front door one morning. AV greeted them and showed them to the balcony, summoning me to fetch them some cold drinks while they chatted in Spanish. After they left I asked AV why they had come. Apparently, to her great amusement, the local police force had got it into their heads the villa was a brothel and she was the Madame. Well that was soon explained when AV showed them our pretty decent artwork as well as our various bits of misshapen pottery. However she explained that they had asked if they could invite two of her girls to the Police Ball which, they said, was to be held that weekend at the Parador on the sea front in Jávea. Naturally enough none of us girls wanted to be seen anywhere with these spectacularly short, ugly, oily haired, garlic and tobacco-ridden middle aged Spanish policemen. But in a rare moment of madness AV had thought it would keep her in favour with the Jávea plod, particularly as she held no license for running a school – art, finishing or otherwise. Unfortunately I was selected to accompany Shortarse 1, but fortunately Jenny from Peru, who spoke fluent Spanish, was chosen for Shortarse 2, (as AV had nicknamed them.)

We got ready without any enthusiasm on the Saturday evening; as we had no evening dresses in Spain, AV lent us two of her genuine saris, kept from her youth in India, and showed us how to put them on. The two policemen came to the villa to collect us as the other girls stood on the terrace and waved us goodbye, giggling mercilessly. Reluctantly we climbed into the back of the police car and had only gone a few yards down the hill towards the village when Jenny, normally so taciturn and shy, abruptly let forth an angry stream of Spanish to the two men in front. The driver slammed on the brakes and the car screeched to a halt. Jenny grabbed my arm, opened the door and dragged me out onto the road. Another profanity from Jenny (a very strong one I had heard AV use) sent the men off down the hill at speed. As we walked back to the villa I asked Jenny what had just happened.

"There was no Police Ball at the Parador or anywhere else," she explained. "They were discussing whose flat they should take us to!"

Since having children of my own I realise what an enormous responsibility it must have been for AV to cope with and look after us wayward girls on her own – her husband having flown home to his own beloved pedigree herd of Jersey cows at Chantry's farm.

As the days grew warmer, we would spend our free afternoons sunbathing on the roof terrace or walking through the orange groves to the pebble beach by the marina where we could swim.

We were all determined to get suntans and, in the hope of bleaching our hair, we sat for hours in the sun with our hair soaked in fresh lemon juice and our fair skin smothered in olive oil; all we needed was a sprinkling of seasoning. In the middle of the orange groves nearby was a small discothèque with the remains of a windmill rising from one end. *El Moli Blanc* was frequented by the local youth and was only open at weekends; AV forbad us to go, fearing what nine nubile girls might get up to if we came into close contact with the Spanish boys. By chance we discovered that AV took a sleeping pill each night as soon as she thought we were all safely tucked up in our beds. Thereafter we feigned exhaustion every Saturday evening and, with dressing gowns covering our mini dresses, we said our goodnights to her before retiring to our ground floor bedrooms where we waited impatiently for the upstairs lights to go out. The doors of the villa were locked each night, their keys safely on AV's bedside table, so we used to climb out of our bedroom windows and jump down to the ground below.

It took about half an hour to walk through the orange groves to the disco, where we happily danced the night away with each other and some of the local boys until it closed in the early hours. Meandering back through the moonlit groves was a pleasure I will never forget, picking a few of the enormous fruits to eat on the way back to the villa. We happily believed it wasn't stealing, since so many oranges lay unpicked and rotting on the ground between the trees; besides, the temptation was utterly impossible to resist amidst the pervading citrus scent of the fruit trees. Miraculously AV never discovered what we had been up to on these Saturday night escapades until long after we left Spain, when UP had returned to holiday at the villa as soon as our final term ended. The following Christmas my parents and I were invited to a reunion party at Chantry. UP came straight up to me and, after a hug and a kiss, asked me to lift up my foot. I couldn't understand why, but did as I was asked.

"Hmm," said UP, quizzically studying the sole of my shoe. "Size 5, should I think you are?"

"Yes Uncle Peter, I'm normally a size 5," I replied innocently, imagining that he and AV perhaps planned a gift of some new shoes.

"Last summer Pablo the gardener showed me some footprints he'd found in the baked earth below your bedroom window," he chuckled, peering at me questioningly with his twinkly blue eyes. "I just wanted to see if the sizes matched."

Naturally I pretended I couldn't imagine what on earth he was talking about and luckily he didn't question me further, but I knew he had rumbled us. AV only took her pupils to her villa once more after my year and she wasn't as lucky as she had been with us. One of the girls that year came back to England expecting a half-Spanish baby …

* * *

With such happy memories to look back on, Jávea and the surrounding Marina Alta region was the natural choice for us to find a perfect home for our little family for the next two years. Jeremy had rented a villa for us until we could find somewhere to buy, so we now had something concrete to look forward to as we began to pack up our home. My parents came to help and together we filled box after box, labelled *Spain* or *Storage*; others were marked for a garage sale or charity shop and anything beyond redemption ended up in a skip. Some items such

as Rory's larger toys, Miranda's spare cot, assorted summer baby
clothes, a year's supply of disposable nappies, baby powder (unavailable in Spain), and all the paraphernalia needed for a three
month-old baby had already been taken to Moraira on Seahawk.
Rory had broken up from the twee private school in Kingsbridge
to where he would never have to return; I think he was as relieved as were we. Instead he was booked into a small international school in Jávea, founded and run by two English teachers
who had moved to Spain with their families, where he would
be taught in Spanish in the mornings and in English during the
afternoons.

Our home of three years sold very quickly and we had already
booked a family suite at the Thurlestone Hotel from the day
of completion until our departure to Spain in mid-December.
Jeremy would be leaving first as he was driving our car to Spain
and would meet us there; my parents were flying with me, the
children and Lucinda so we could all be together for Christmas.
On the day we left the house for the last time the new owner
turned up at the front door late in the afternoon while I was
feeding Miranda in my bedroom. We had not expected him
until the following morning and my dressing table still had to
be packed. I could hear our purchaser's voice as he brought his
luggage and various bits of furniture into the hall in his tactless
haste to move in. To my dismay Jeremy came into the room
with a cardboard box and began throwing in the contents of the
dressing table faster than I could retrieve my essential make-up.

"You'll just have to come as you are," he insisted, as the odious
new owner's voice grew louder and closer. "He wants us out of
the house now, and anyway we're booked for an early supper at
the hotel so we can all eat together,"

"Jeremy, don't you dare let him come in here!" I squeaked, rapidly trying to extricate Miranda and gather the last few bits from my dressing table. "Why on earth has the beastly man come today?"

"He obviously isn't a man of his word," Jeremy concluded. "Although the house has officially belonged to him since midday, so I suppose he has every right."

It was a terribly upsetting way to leave: I had no time say goodbye to the home we had built, loved and enjoyed for the last three years, but perhaps that was for the best. Jeremy had already hired a removal lorry and packed the whole thing himself with the bulk of our furniture and belongings; the following day he would be driving up to rural West Sussex and unloading it all into a wing of his parents' house until it was needed. We were welcomed warmly by our friends whose family owned the hotel, and shown to a spacious family room overlooking the gardens and sea beyond. After changing we went to the restaurant for supper, Miranda sleeping peacefully in her pram beside me. The hotel had been elaborately decorated for Christmas and the food was absolutely delicious, especially the Strawberry Cheesecake; to our utter amazement Rory, a notoriously fussy eater at that age, polished off his portion and asked for a second helping. I was so delighted that I asked the chef for the recipe, which I have to this day. (Take 2 gallons of double cream, 8 pounds of butter, 20 tubs of cream cheese, a barrel of icing sugar, etc ... I never did manage to reduce it into sensible quantities.)

The next few days at the hotel were a godsend, Rory and I made good use of the indoor pool and we all went for walks along the windswept beach with my parents, who by then lived a stone's throw from Thurlestone Sands. Of course they were devastated by our decision to move to Spain, but they did understand this was our last opportunity to take a sabbatical for many years. I hoped the edge would be taken off their disappointment by joining us in Jávea for Christmas.

Jeremy had already left on the ferry from Plymouth to Spain by the time the rest of us assembled at Totnes railway station with a mountain of luggage. My mother had arranged with British Rail for my father to have assistance for the journey, as his heart condition made it difficult for him to walk very far. We had to disembark at Reading for the coach to Heathrow and as the train pulled into the station, Lucinda lifted Miranda and her pram out of the narrow carriage door. Mummy followed with Rory, as did my father who had been met by a porter with a wheelchair. I began hurling our eighteen pieces of luggage onto the platform as best I could, as I watched my mother, the children and our feckless nanny happily following the porter with Pop in the wheelchair towards the exit – all of them totally oblivious to my struggle with the luggage that was still on the train. A guard blew his whistle despite my open door and the train began to move. I was about to be whisked on towards London with half our luggage but without the rest of my family.

"MUMMY!" I screamed as she turned around and realised instantly what was happening.

"STOP THE TRAIN!" she shouted to nobody in particular, racing back to my door and holding it open as she trotted to keep pace with the accelerating train.

Mercifully an alert passenger must have pulled the emergency cord. The train juddered briefly to a halt and a kind gentleman tossed the remaining bags onto the platform as I leapt off the train after them. I was still shaking like a leaf and feeling sick at the prospect of being taken onwards to Paddington. How could I have contacted my family in those far off days before mobile phones? And I was the only one who could feed baby Miranda! We got on the coach in the nick of time but I couldn't stop shaking until we disembarked at Heathrow. I still have recurring nightmares about that journey and always panic at the very mention of a train journey. At the airport another wheelchair with helper was waiting for my father, who led the procession with the rest of us trailing behind with two overloaded trolleys of luggage and Miranda's pram. The old music hall song written in 1919, *My Old Man Said Follow The Van*, which my father had always sung to me when I was little, was playing in my head until we eventually boarded our flight.

Jeremy was waiting for us at Alicante airport and drove us to the villa he had rented in Moraira, having picked up the keys from the agency on the way there. It looked promising as we drove through the gates and parked at the side of the house; Rory was thrilled to glimpse a swimming pool sparkling in the warm sunshine to one side of the gardens, until he realised it was unheated. Opening the front door I thought I had stepped into a mouldy fridge, the entire house feeling bitterly cold and damp. Jeremy stomped in with news that the oil tank was empty, livid that his explicit instructions to heat the house before our arrival had been ignored by the agents. He tore off into Moraira and returned an hour later with a couple of portable gas heaters, three electric fan heaters and the disappointing news that no oil would be delivered until after the weekend – if we were lucky. *Mañana por la mañana* was the Spaniards' well used euphemism for *I don't give a damn if I'm late*, as we would continually discover. (Years later we found it impossible to be angry with the Greeks, who were equally relaxed about punctuality, because they always arrived with a small present or gave a generous discount when they *did* eventually appear. Moreover we had to laugh with them, so imaginative were their excuses. Jeremy thinks I must be mostly Greek as he says I have absolutely no awareness of the passage of time.)

The villa was soon filled with poisonous clouds of gas fumes and steam as I attempted to unpack, so I decided our clothes would stay drier where they were. A heavy dew of condensation quickly formed on the walls and ceilings as the evening grew colder, while steam rose gently from the soft furnishings. After a hasty supper in the village we resigned ourselves to an uncomfortable night in wringing wet beds. Next morning Mummy awoke with a rasping cough; she was prone to bronchitis and I had predicted its onset after our night in the cold, damp house. Jeremy stripped the beds and carried all the mattresses out into the sun, where they steamed like fresh horse droppings on a frosty morning. We sat by the swimming pool in the sun to thaw out and hoped Mummy would feel better. But over the weekend her condition deteriorated and on Monday we took her to a doctor in Moraira, who prescribed strong antibiotics that we were able to buy immediately from the pharmacy. We felt dreadfully guilty but she was brave and uncomplaining and assured us it wasn't our fault. Things eventually improved when the central heating oil arrived, although the wardrobes and cupboards clung determinedly to their dapplings of mildew.

As Christmas approached we decorated the villa with a few coloured baubles and ropes of tinsel bought in the outdoor market, although Christmas trees had long since sold out. On Boxing Day we joined forces with our friends from Salcombe who were spending Christmas in Moraira at their parents' comfortable villa, to where we had all been invited for lunch. It was a blessing to feel properly warm and dry for an entire afternoon.

On New Year's Eve we held a party at our villa and invited our Salcombe friends. My mother helped me make canapés and a cold buffet, which we laid on the long dining table. Lucinda looked after Rory and Miranda while we made the preparations, but disappeared for what seemed like hours after tea. I was getting cross because I wanted to have time to shower and change before our guests arrived for supper. Mummy went upstairs to call Lucinda and found her ironing a load of her own clothes in her bedroom. I began to have doubts about her suitability from that night on, particularly when she went straight to bed without helping to us clear up after our guests had left. I warned her we would be leaving quite early the next morning and asked her to ready everything for a day out with Rory and Miranda: drinks and swimming things for Rory, spare clothes for both children, baby changing bag, nappies and so on.

New Year's Day dawned bright, warm and sunny with clear blue skies, so we decided to go to Benidorm for lunch. We had heard all the scathing reports about this holiday enclave and decided we should see for ourselves just how ghastly it really was. I got myself and the children ready, but there was no sign of Lucinda. We were all ready and waiting to leave, having called her an hour beforehand, and once again she was in her room, still in her nightie with nothing packed for the children. She casually informed Jeremy she had been invited to spend the day with our friends from the previous evening, who would be coming to collect her later. We were not best pleased.

The beach at Benidorm, a five mile stretch of golden sand divided at its centre by the Old Town, we found stunningly beautiful. Running the length of the beach was an attractively paved promenade, interspersed with enormous palm trees. The only people strolling there that day were Spaniards, dressed in all their finery, jewellery and fur coats against the cruel desolation of a warm, windless winter's day. We lunched in a small fish restaurant opposite the prom, gazing at the view of the sparkling sea and trying to imagine the little village before fishing had fallen into decline in the 1950s. Afterwards we sat on the beach while Rory gamely ran in and out of the water in his swimming trunks. There was only one drawback: if you nonchalantly gazed over your shoulder and away from the sea you were instantly slapped in the face by the continuous cliff of concrete that hemmed the entire bay. The hideous multi-storey apartment blocks and hotels blocked all view of the hills of the Sierra Gelada behind; even the famous Puig Campana mountain was hidden. Nearly all of this had been built after I had been in Jávea with AV and the girls, when Benidorm and Calpe had still been quaint, largely unspoilt fishing villages at heart. This hideous building work has continued and by 2002 the highest structure in Benidorm was the logically named Gran Hotel Bali, standing 186 metres tall with 50 floors and 776 rooms to accommodate 2,000 guests; I imagine there is no Gran Hotel Benidorm in Bali. Worse has since followed. Was Benidorm in an earthquake zone, I wondered?

Next morning while I was feeding Miranda in bed, Jeremy was busily scanning advertisements in the local paper for houses for sale in the area; it was a weekly routine that had so far produced nothing but grunts of disapproval from him. We had viewed several properties since our arrival without any success for one reason or another; perhaps it was time to broaden our search before disillusionment set in.

"This one looks rather promising," he suddenly announced, reading it out to me, "and it's jolly reasonably priced too. *For Sale: 200 year-old finca, sensitively modernised with separate casita and swimming pool. Set amidst its own productive land in a tranquil valley of orange and almond groves near Jesús Pobre.* "

"I know exactly where that is," I exclaimed. "We used to buy bread there when I was with AV; the village bakery made the best bread and cakes for miles around. Call the number right away!"

Jeremy has always thought it highly inconsiderate to make telephone calls – even to close friends – before nine in the morning; the same peculiar discipline applied to coffee time, lunch time, teatime, drinks time and suppertime, or for that matter, after nine in the evening. This policy, which suited my telephone averse husband very well, usually meant that whomever he wanted to call was unavailable, because they were busily doing all the things people had to do when they weren't at home. Eventually, and only after much clock watching, he made the call to the advertiser and we arranged to view the property the following day. For better or worse an old finca near Jesús Pobre seemed destined to be ours.

Matters with Lucinda came to a head on the day of our appointment with the lawyers in Jávea, where we were due to sign the purchase documents for the finca. I had asked Lucinda to have herself and the children ready by nine o'clock next morning, in plenty of time to get to our meeting in Jávea. I was already in the car with both children, having given them breakfast and packed their bags myself. When Lucinda didn't appear, Jeremy left the car and went back into the villa and knocked on Lucinda's door, only to discover she was still in her dressing gown and was once again ironing her own clothes.

"We can't wait a moment longer," he warned before closing the front door. "So I'm afraid you'll have to stay behind this time! We shan't be long."

Halfway to our appointment Jeremy suddenly remembered the front door was fitted with an automatic deadlock. Our nanny was locked in, but as she was unlikely to have got herself ready before our planned return two hours later, I wasn't unduly worried; as far as I was concerned she could continue ironing her clothes and daydreaming in peace. On our return we found the villa empty, an open window on the ground floor telling us all we needed to know. A quick call to our friends in Moraira found Lucinda safe and well, having walked down the hill to find them. Apparently she was now so traumatised after being left on her own for two hours that she wanted to remain with our friends and return to England with them a few days later. It all sounded rather contrived and we came to the conclusion that Lucinda had already decided life with us in Spain wasn't really her cup of tea. Likewise we had many doubts about her reliability as a nanny, however proficient she might have been with a steam iron and boiling water. Her departure was for the best, although at the time we thought we might miss another pair of hands to help with the children during the trips we intended to take on the boat. As it turned out we managed very well indeed; Rory was bright and well behaved and Miranda was a very easy baby; they both took to life afloat like ducklings to water.

After taking Mummy and Pop to Alicante Airport and waving them a sorrowful farewell, Jeremy and I found ourselves alone with our two young children in an unfamiliar country, where the only people we knew were Roy and Gill, the charming couple who had sold us the finca on behalf of Gill's brother. Although quite a bit older than us, it was a comfort to know we could call on them if ever we needed help or advice. Set on a hill their elegant villa looked down our valley to Jesús Pobre and the three ruined windmills; with a powerful telescope I would probably be able to wave to them when we moved into La Abubilla.

Our little family of four willingly gave up the rented villa and moved onto Seahawk for a few weeks until our furniture arrived from England. When it rained we had to dash along the dock from the car and negotiate the passerelle between the cockpit and the quay, a tricky task with a babe in arms, a pram and bags of shopping. But once on board we were soon warm, dry and lacked for nothing, even when the decks were covered in frost or awash with rain.

We moved into La Abubilla on a crystal clear morning at the beginning of February. As Jeremy organised our furniture and opened the dozens of packing cases, I began to explore our new surroundings, pushing Miranda in her pram. Rory was thrilled to have his red go-kart once again and pedalled ahead of us, swerving from one side of the dusty track to the other as we made our progress past our little vineyard and through the orange and lemon groves under the warm sunshine. Each neatly pruned lemon tree sparkled with pure white blossom, shown to perfection against the glossy dark green leaves and ripening fruits, which looked as if they were made of shiny yellow porcelain. I never got over the thrill of seeing oranges and lemons actually growing on trees; for me it was worth returning to Spain just to witness this miracle again. Tidy rows of trees in the groves stretched as far as the eye could see in all directions, their bright fruits glowing against the shiny leaves like glass balls on a Christmas tree. The verges of rough grasses on either side of the track were already sprouting aromatic wild herbs and a variety of wild flowers; ox eye daisies rubbed shoulders with tiny purple orchids and glittering yellow buttercups. Elsewhere the almond trees were a vision of delicate pale pink blossom and every few yards the fronds of a mature date palm whispered in the light Spring breeze. The earth was the same warm red as the familiar soil of South Devon and soon our shoes were permanently covered in a fine red dust.

It was only as the sun sank behind the mountain range in the late afternoon that the full fragrance of the citrus groves began to waft over us, drifting in waves of deliciousness so heady you could taste it. As the evenings drew out we made a ritual of taking our evening glasses of wine into the garden to sit by the pool, enveloped in the scents of late lemon blossom, watching the sun slip behind the countless folds of my Elephant Hills on the western horizon before the cooler air began to fall. I had named the hills after their uniform shape and colouring, rounded and grey like the backs of a distant herd of elephants; fuzzy outlines of sparse vegetation on the skyline looked exactly like the coarse hair found on the animals.

Before the family awoke each morning I would slip outside with my first cup of Earl Grey and wander around the garden in my dressing gown, sniffing appreciatively at the scents of the waking Spanish day. Higher up the valley coffee was brewing and the delicious aroma of freshly roasting beans and baking bread rolled gently down through the trees. The gardens were not overlooked, a high dense hedge of pink and white oleander ably dividing the finca from our nearest neighbour, a Spanish smallholder. On the first morning I was in a peaceful reverie as I meandered along the path to the casita, only the crunching of dry white gravel under my slippers disturbing a blissful silence. Beside the oleander hedge, its bright flowers glinting like pink rubies in the early light, I began studying the extraordinary prickly pear, or Barbary fig tree, which stood ten feet tall near the casita on the boundary of our land. To me the strange, round formations covered in cactus spines – which are actually its leaves – resembled the felt ears of a child's toy rabbit that had been stuck haphazardly onto a gnarled tree trunk; they protruded at every conceivable angle, some growing upon the next, here and there adorned with crimson fruits growing from the edges of the leaves like thorny pimples.

I was contemplating this primitive plant and wondering if it would be worth risking its sharp spines to pick the fruit, when a sudden noise shocked me out of my daydream. I can only describe it as a loud guttural honking followed by snorting and coughing, culminating with a highly energetic hawking. Could it be an animal? A wild boar perhaps? I heard they had been seen in the valley and I stood frozen to the spot, wondering if I should keep perfectly still or turn on my heel and race back into the house. I held my breath, then a few seconds later the repertoire was repeated. Gingerly I crept towards the sound, which appeared to be coming from the other side of the oleanders. Attempting to peer through the thick foliage, I leapt out of my skin as the third encore erupted right in front of me. I must have gasped and given myself away, as a gruff voice came through the bushes.

I was so taken aback all I could say was a hasty 'Cómo dice, Señor?', realising no Spanish lady could have possibly made these repulsive noises with such a deep voice. Then I remembered another phrase learnt at the age of seventeen when I was last in Spain.

"Hola Señor, cuál es su nombre?"

"Manuel," my neighbour appeared to grunt amid yet more coughing.

I waited for the return question, which never came, and heard him shuffling back towards his little shack behind a thicket of thorns and trees. Every morning Spitting Manuel performed the same throat clearing ritual with varying levels of gusto in precisely the same place; I began to wonder if he waited close to our hedge to startle me, knowing I would be in the garden at that time, although Jeremy suspected it was more likely the favoured spot for Manuel to relieve himself as he probably had done for the past seventy years. I never got more than a reluctant, indecipherable grunt out of him, even when I passed him on the goat path as I walked with the children. In this land of the late lamented spittoon, I was often tempted to offer him a large box of Kleenex.

A lookalike, who must have been Manuel's slightly younger brother, although stooped from years tending the vines, was positively garrulous by comparison. Early in the summer mornings he occasionally pegged his way along the track behind our house as he made his painfully slow progress towards the village, often pausing to rest on the rim of our well, where he invariably took the opportunity to clear his airways *con brio*. If ever he caught sight of Jeremy or me through the open doors of our bedroom balcony he would offer his own distinctive salutation.

"Nasty days!" he would heartily call out, shaking his heavily knotted walking stick in the general direction of the clear blue skies above us. Puzzling as it was, we eventually deciphered his peculiar greeting as a slushy, local vernacular for *buenos días.* Forever after Jeremy and I adopted *nasty days!* as our own salutation to each other whenever and wherever we awoke to a perfectly cloudless sky.

Jeremy and I had grown too accustomed to the effusive friendliness and generous hospitality of the Greek Cypriots during the two years we had lived amongst them in Cyprus; it came as quite a rude awakening to find the Spaniards in our valley so indifferent, if not entirely standoffish. This disappointing situation never changed a jot in the following months, try as we might to address our fellow villagers in their own language and thus open a small doorway into their community. In fairness to them we rarely came across anyone of our own age and we never did make much headway with their coarse dialect, so unrestrained mingling was never a likely outcome.

Early in January Rory began his first term at the Lady Elizabeth School in Jávea. Shoehorned into a modest townhouse it would soon outgrow, the school was founded by two English teachers who had retired early to sunny Spain only to find they missed the activity and satisfaction of their former lives. Aware of a large expat community of English speaking parents in the area, whose only option hitherto was to send their children to Spanish schools, they had opened their fledgling international school the previous Autumn. Rory had been enrolled for the Spring term before we left England and had been lucky to find a vacancy. In his new school's winter uniform of a royal blue jumper over a crisp white shirt, grey trousers, grey ankle socks and brown leather shoes, Rory looked adorable; it was so much more practical and comfortable than the depressingly formal green blazer and striped tie of his school in Kingsbridge. We all bundled into the car to take him to school on his first day; I was far more nervous than he was. With Rory and I gaily singing along to Spanish children's songs from a cassette we had bought to help him master the language, we drew up at the school gates in the brilliant January sunshine. We can both still sing those songs thirty-seven years later.

A cluster of children were chatting happily in the garden and Rory was out of the car before I could say 'Olé!' His teacher was there to greet him and to introduce him to the only other boy in her class; luckily Mrs. Jones was heaven sent as she had a teenage son of her own and understood boys, assuring me that she much preferred boys to girls since they were far less complicated. If a boy had an argument with another boy it was soon settled with no hard feelings, whereas, in her opinion, girls were 'catty', spiteful and held grudges for months. It was such a pity the head of Rory's first school had held the opposite opinion and couldn't cope with Rory's mischievous exuberance.

In the afternoon we collected a very excited little boy; all the way home in the car he chatted happily about his first day. He had instantly made friends with Adam, the only other boy in his class, whose English parents owned a video hire shop. From what we could gather they had become a gang of two and had successfully held their own against the little girls at break times.

Rory had a passion for anything electrical or mechanical – just like his father. He loved the Meccano sets his grandparents bought him for Christmas and birthdays and was never much interested in non-technical toys … although a funny thing did happen when Miranda was born. To celebrate her birth, she was given an expensive Teddy Bear from some very generous friends who lived nearby. The bear was large and soft, with *Harrods 1987* embroidered on the sole of one foot; but as soon as the bear was unwrapped Rory looked at it enviously and after briefly showing it to baby Miranda, he announced that he would take it to his bedroom 'to look after it' for his sister until she was older. It stayed in Rory's room for years but I have it now, safely tucked away in my bedroom until it may be needed again one day.

During the mornings the children were taught in Spanish by a local teacher, in the afternoons the classes were in English. Rory picked up his new language quickly and easily, I would take him shopping so he could translate for me. One of his words shocked Jeremy to the core when I yelled it at an over-enthusiastic fishmonger at the market in Jávea as he scooped hundreds of Rory's favourite fresh whitebait into a plastic bag.

"BASTANTE!" (Enough) I shouted, as Jeremy looked at me askance.

My Spanish was rather rusty, after all it had been 15 years since I had learnt the language at AV's villa in Jávea. Jeremy was far more disciplined, with his natural flair for languages, he studied from books at night and practised with the workmen we employed to build the balustrades and extended terraces around our swimming pool. As Spring burst upon the valley and the days became warmer, our life fell into a pleasant routine in this sunny, fragrant, flower and fruit filled corner of the world. At precisely seven o'clock every morning a resident Hoopoe took up his favourite position on the top of one of our flowering agaves by the swimming pool. His distinctive call, *hoop, hoop-hoop, hoop*, served as our alarm to get up and take Rory to school in time for early morning assembly.

The agave only flowers after many years of growth, after which the plant dies and is replaced by baby plants that have self seeded around its giant base. The plants are positively prehistoric looking and one can imagine dinosaurs meandering between them. The huge, needle-pointed leaves have serrated edges covered in lethally sharp thorns to discourage any unwanted attention. When Jeremy's mother came to stay I had been surprised to find her up at first light, busily going from one agave to the next with her nail scissors, meticulously cutting off every single thorn and spike at Rory's eye level; she had become obsessed with a terrifying premonition that he would run into them whilst playing and be blinded for life. I fully expect the agave's leaves to evolve further until they become completely and literally pointless, thanks to the unwanted attentions of overprotective grandmothers.

AV used to say Spain was a cold country with hot sun, an observation that was certainly true in the early Spring. It brought to mind Charles Dickens' description from *Great Expectations*:

'*It was one of those March days when the sun shines hot and the wind blows cold: when it is summer in the light, and winter in the shade.*'

Rory had his own ingenious way of dressing for this unusual climate. Finding the sun too hot for his liking, even in early Spring, he also decided the wind was often chill and the terracotta floors in the finca distinctly cold. Rory solved this problem by wearing a large scarlet sombrero on his head and his red après-ski boots on his feet.

Every morning Miranda took a nap in her pram in the shady courtyard, lulled to sleep by the delicate whispering of the date palm fronds wafting in the warm breeze, the birdsong, the rasping of the cicadas and the soporific humming of squadrons of

© *Jani Tully Chaplin*

bees in the oleander hedges surrounding our garden. It was difficult not to doze off in such a place. The warmth of the morning
sun on the dew damp, fertile red earth and the citrus groves all
around us in the valley created an aromatic scent that mingled
with the distinctive notes of wild fennel, thyme, oregano and
jasmine. It was a heady combination that none of the greatest
perfume houses in Paris had been able to replicate. The almond
trees beyond the swimming pool cast their cool green shade on
the ground beneath, their dainty leaves shimmering like shoals
of tiny fish in an underwater world, providing the only place
in the garden where grass would grow. One such tree was very

special, if slightly incongruous, it grew beside the steps to the swimming pool. In early spring it sprouted little pale pink tufts of blossom, but only on its left hand side, so we knew it was an almond tree. Then quite suddenly a few days later it produced some completely different flowers on the right hand side, much smaller and almost white, which I was sure belonged to the cherry family. Watching the slow progress of this strange tree with interest, we were amazed to see the velvety green almonds developing alongside some dark green fruits.

We asked our gardener Miguel about the tree. With much gesticulating as he realised our knowledge of horticultural Spanish was sadly lacking, he explained that a plum tree had been grafted to an almond. He must have thought us very dense as we slowly struggled to grasp his meaning and in exasperation, he ended up clasping a branch from each species in a loving embrace and shouting: "*Dos arboles!*" (Two trees). Miguel was a gentle soul from La Mancha who spoke with a Castilian accent we could actually understand; even so our vocabulary hadn't been up to the task.

Growing in the shade of a heavy curtain of bougainvillea that overhung the naya and courtyard was a large exotic datura, with enormous heart shaped leaves. In the early summer it produced massive, pendulous flowers, the white elongated bells dangled from the greenery, their petals curling up at the bottom like Edwardian lampshades. The scent from these flowers was overpoweringly heady, similar to *magnolia grandiflora*, but we sniffed them with care and without touching them as they were poisonous. Squat, bushy date palms grew everywhere in the area, at this time of year weighed down by long stems of bright orange dates, like golden bullets. Hearing them referred to as dates, Rory decided to try one, but biting into the rock hard, unripe fruit he discovered a taste so bitter he spat it out immediately and declared it absolutely disgusting. To his disappointment it was nothing like the soft, sweet, sticky brown variety he remembered from Christmases past.

Clumps of tall, sweet smelling iris sprouted in every garden, their deep blue and purple jewel colours forming a rich tapestry with the golden yellow of winter flowering jasmine, scarlet and purple bougainvillea and the dark, inky-green of the Cypress trees that were planted in long straight rows, like toy soldiers, to form windbreaks for the fruit groves. Miguel lovingly tended our moscatel vines, as he had done for enough years to consider them his own; vines can be temperamental and we thought it best to leave them in his capable, calloused hands. A mutually beneficial arrangement was continued with him, whereby he cared for the vines and took the grapes at harvest time. We were assured we could anticipate a bottle or two of our very own sweet wine before Christmas, but perhaps fortuitously this expectation never materialised.

But it was comforting to know our vines were being well cared for as we watched Miguel's diminutive figure hunched over the neat rows of stumpy, deformed looking plants. In his faded blue cotton jacket and trousers, and shaded by a frayed straw hat the size of a bicycle wheel, he shuffled about muttering and humming tunelessly to himself in the sun. I imagined his wife wrapping a chunk of crusty bread, some leathery Serrano ham and a lump of hard cheese in a clean cloth for him to take as sustenance for his day's toil ahead; a carafe of thin red wine, enclosed in woven basketwork for portability, would always be included. It amazed me to see the labourers swilling back quantities of young wine first thing in the morning as part of their breakfast. Often to be seen sitting at the edges of fields, on pavements, building sites or harbour walls, they enjoyed their alcohol without over-indulgence and seemed perfectly capable of working afterwards. Could this explain their carefree, casual and decidedly cavalier attitude to work and the passage of time, we wondered.

Our own prejudices about Spanish wines, formed in the infamous days when migraine-inflicting plonk was imported during the 1970s, initially led Jeremy towards the expensive end of the supermarket shelves. Working his way down to the cheapest offers, and only after many bottles had been poured down the drain, he at last found a light Vouvray style white for the equivalent of sixty pence per litre bottle; it was deliciously drinkable and eagerly awaited as soon as the sun dipped over the yard-arm. Excessively chilled and generously poured into goblets of the local, palest green recycled glass, the wine eminently suited the ambience and climate of our rural surroundings; strangely enough it was no less acceptable on board Seahawk at lunch-time, although I doubt the bottles would have been potable if uncorked in England. Our friend Tim said it must have been made with antifreeze to sell at such a low price, (there had been a great scandal in Austria two years earlier), and Jeremy wonders to this day if any glycol in that wine was responsible for him permanently shivering in any climate less than tropical. We certainly did drink rather a lot of it.

The pool grew warmer with each passing day, allowing us all to swim at every opportunity. Jeremy was incapable of sitting idle and always found more jobs to do, sometimes on Seahawk, but he enjoyed the pool as much as the rest of us between chores.

Rory wore an ingenious swimming suit with polystyrene floats inserted into pockets around the chest; these were surreptitiously removed one at a time over a few days until Rory suddenly found himself swimming unaided. We had bought a special rubber ring for Miranda in England; it had a back support and a panel underneath with two holes for her legs to go through. She adored this ring and soon learnt to paddle her little legs to propel herself around in the warm water with surprising agility. Lunch was taken under a garden parasol by the pool and afternoon tea was served in the naya when it became too hot to sit in the open. Rory was home from school by four each day and immediately jumped into the pool, having demolished a snack and a cold drink in the car on the way back.

One very warm Sunday towards the end of March I decided to make a start on cleaning and preparing the casita, where Jeremy's parents would be staying when they arrived in a few days time. Dry leaves littered the tiled floors and the simple furniture was covered in layers of fine red dust blown in from the fields whenever the rooms had been aired. The casita hadn't been occupied for several years, but it was bone dry and free from any trace of mildew even if the veils of cobwebs reminded me of Miss Haversham's house. By far the worst cleaning job was the loo; its white bowl was badly stained and the cracked plastic seat wobbled and slid about so badly that any user would likely be thrown off like a cowboy in a bucking bronco contest. I would have plenty of time to buy a nice new seat from the the excellent *ferreteria* in Jávea, so that was not a problem. Miranda was asleep in her pram in the ample shade of the date palm in the courtyard, Rory was charging around on his go-kart, Jeremy was in a trench laying a new cable to the pool house and my rubber-gloved arm was halfway down the pan with a scouring pad and lashings of bleach as the phone rang in the house.

"Jeremy!" I yelled, "Take the phone!"

A telephone in our rural part of Spain was a great novelty and an essential asset in the days before mobile phones; some new-comers had to wait years to get a line connected and its presence had been another excellent reason to buy our finca with such little hesitation. I carried on scrubbing until Jeremy appeared in the doorway.

"Er," he wavered – never a good sign where Jeremy was con-cerned; any hesitancy usually meant there was something he didn't want to tell me.

"Oh for heaven's sake, what is it? Who was on the phone?"

"Well, you'll never guess …", he began in a dither.

"I haven't got time for guessing games," I answered tetchily between clenched teeth. "I must get all this done before Miranda wakes up for her next feed!"

"It was my mother."

"Oh that's nice of her to call," I replied innocently. "How far have they got into France now?"

"Actually they're at a service station ten minutes away," he re-plied, running back towards the house without waiting to hear my pithy reply.

I was filthy, dripping with exertion and the heat of the warm afternoon, in my very oldest shorts and tee shirt, with hair that needed washing and nails that needed painting – all the things I was planning to do before the arrival of my in-laws at the end of the week. But now they were nearly here, just minutes away. I hadn't shopped for a couple of days so there was little food in the house, having carefully planned to shop for a delicious menu before their arrival in a few days' time. But now there was nothing except oranges, tomatoes, olives, eggs, bread and a fresh batch of Miranda's home made mush – a sloppy, sludge green and very unappetising looking purée of fresh vegetables bought at the local market, all cooked and whizzed up in my liquidiser with a healthy touch of garlic and olive oil.

(I could never give Miranda any of the prepared Spanish baby food because every jar, including the savoury flavours, contained a staggering eighty percent sugar. At cafés I often noticed doting Spanish mothers stirring two large spoonfuls of white sugar into their babies' bottles of milk. No wonder so many Spanish children looked on the chubby side. Whenever we went out for morning coffee with Rory, he had been delighted to find two packets of sugar and a spoon on the saucer of his mug of hot chocolate – until I whipped the packets away. Rory loathed the Spanish milk and refused to drink it until my mother sent supplies of strawberry flavoured Nesquik from England to disguise the taste; as this powder contained mainly saccharine instead of sugar, I consoled myself that I was at least getting milk into my growing son.)

"Mummy," came a small distracting voice from the doorway as I stripped off my Marigolds and wondered what on earth to do first – there was no time left for any more cleaning. Luckily I had made up the beds in the casita with clean linen and put new towels in the bathroom, but a new loo seat would just have to wait.

"What is it Rory? Nana and Mike-Mike are nearly here!" (Rory's pet names, invented when he was learning to talk.)

Whatever he wanted, I knew the thought of his adored

grandmother's imminent arrival would instantly distract him and that he would race to the drive and await their approaching car.

"I've done something awful to Miranda," his voice unnaturally quiet and scared. "Come quickly."

"What on earth have you done now?" I shouted as I ran after him towards the naya where I had left Miranda peacefully sleeping in its cool shade.

The pram was lying on its side in the middle of the paved courtyard and there was no sound to be heard from within. My heart stopped. I flew to the pram and saw Miranda looking up at me, smiling happily and seemingly uninjured. I lifted her out as Rory righted the pram.

"How did this happen?" I asked my shocked son, his large brown eyes like saucers in his pale face.

"Well, I was just whizzing the pram round and round and she liked it, but then it fell over and I thought I'd killed her."

"Never mind all that now. Just go and keep an eye out for Nana and Mike-Mike's car," I snapped.

There was no time to give the matter a second thought while I concentrated on the next drama, at the same time remembering to bless our invaluable telephone line; I couldn't begin to imagine how much worse it would have been if my in-law's had turned up without any notice whatsoever.

Rushing back into the house and depositing Miranda in her baby walker, I took a very quick shower and found a change of clothes; my hair would just have to wait. Rory called out a few minutes later to tell us he had spotted Liz and Michael's car winding its way down the narrow track between the orange groves towards La Abubilla, where Jeremy and I calmly greeted them as if we hadn't a care in the world. They were both tired and hungry, Michael having driven through France and Spain like a rally driver and refusing to stop anywhere for the night or even for a proper meal. Liz apologetically asked if we had anything they could eat, as they had survived largely on a lump of cheddar and four apples brought from Sussex. I dispatched Jeremy into the kitchen to make tea and to find some biscuits while I showed them to the casita.

"When you've had a little rest we're going out to eat this evening," I explained, hoping they would both fall asleep and give me time to wash my hair, tidy our house, feed and bath Miranda, and get Rory showered and changed into something presentable for our outing.

"Out for supper!" I heard my shocked mother-in-law exclaim behind me as I ran back to the house. "Why on earth would we want to go *out for supper?*"

Instead of resting, Michael decided to turn his car around and reverse it nearer to the casita, a manoeuvre that flattened a section of oleander hedge and sent part of the stone capping around our well crashing into the water below. Satisfied he had dented the last two remaining panels hitherto unblemished, (and deciding therefore that a brand new car was now fully justified), he planted himself in our sitting room with his two day-old copy of *The Daily Telegraph*. On his way between car and sofa he had walked over the pile of damp red earth beside Jeremy's trench, nonchalantly treading a meandering trail of mud-caked footprints over every inch of our brand new cream rugs. The stains never did come out.

Luckily there was a charming traditional Spanish restaurant on the slopes of Montgó, its sheltered terrace offering gloriously panoramic views towards the Jalon Valley. At this time of year, from February to April, framed by the distant Elephant Hills, the valley was a misty sea of almond blossom; Spaniards, foreign residents and visitors came from miles around to view the spectacle, much as the Japanese do during the cherry blossom season. With Miranda sleeping in her pram beside our table and Rory chattering happily to his grandmother, supper was an unexpected success. This was very fortunate for all concerned, as I planned to inflict my sparse culinary skills on them the following day when I had found time to visit the shops.

Early next morning Liz and I left the children with Jeremy and drove to the shops in Jávea. I intended to impress my in-laws with a delicious dish of Paella. I bought a selection of salad vegetables, rice and some fresh prawns, but then had to bite the bullet and go to the poultry section of the supermercado for the chicken. (The name is a contradiction in terms as there was nothing super about it. It was small, with sparsely stocked shelves and only one or two staff). I have always loathed butchers' shops and anything to do with raw meat, however you can't make Paella with vegetables, prawns and rice alone, so I had no choice. Nobody in Jávea seemed to speak English in those far off days, so I asked the butcher in my best Spanish for a fresh chicken. He always used to smile crookedly when I used my stumbling Spanish to ask for anything. He held up a ghastly looking pimply old bird complete with head lolling on its scrawny, dangling neck; its poor yellow feet were clenched tight, no doubt from the shock of being so rudely dispatched. I wanted to run away when the butcher asked me what I intended to do with the chicken. Whenever he spoke to me he always shouted, much as the average Englishman abroad tends to do in an attempt to make himself understood, so everyone else in the shop realised that *La Inglésa* was practising her appalling Spanish again.

"Bury it with full military honours?", I muttered, before blurting out "Paella!"

"You want it chopped, Señora? *Picado?*" He asked in Spanish, waving his cleaver menacingly in the air.

Now I was *really* upset. It had come as a horrible shock when returning to Spain as a young mother to find myself addressed as 'Señora' instead of the charming and far more flattering 'Señorita'.

"Si, por favor," I replied, thinking that might save me a lot of time and trouble.

Then to our astonishment the butcher set about the chicken with his cleaver in a frenzied attack that splintered the carcass in a few sickening, blood spattering seconds. I almost fainted. Even my mother-in-law gasped in horror. Satisfied with his handiwork the butcher scraped the battered chicken into a plastic bag and handed it to me – yellow feet, red combed head and all. On the way home Liz said the dessicated chicken wouldn't be safe for any of us to eat, especially for Rory, as it would be full of tiny shards of splintered bones. I suggested we throw it all away, but Liz had lived through all the privations of the blitz and would never throw anything away until it was rotten enough to find its own way to the dustbin. Instead she spent several hours picking through the gore with her tweezers and removing every last fragment of bone she could find. That night Rory ate beans on toast and I had the same; Miranda devoured her fresh mush followed by plain yoghurt, while the three other Chaplins bravely tackled the Paella.

Nobody died but I never made Paella again.

Chapter 5 – Jeremy
Great Minds ... Fools Seldom ...

Over every mountain there is a path, although it may not be seen from the valley.

Theodore Roethke

From my point of view the move to our new home in Spain had been surprisingly straightforward. My personal opinions about the location and style of property we should buy had been clear from the day Jani had first mentioned the idea. To me there seemed little point in living in a foreign country in order to surround oneself with a selection of fellow compatriots who, generally speaking, would not pass the time of day with each other if they were in England. Ideally I didn't much want to be surrounded by anyone, an intransigent position which ruled out great swathes of the Costa Blanca. We soon discovered that long stretches of the entire Spanish coastline were informally out of bounds to the English, for they had already been parcelled up into offshore empires of one northern European country or another, forming loosely partitioned areas specifically annexed by German, Dutch, French or Scandinavian citizens. Any one of these enclaves would have been more preferable to me than life amongst throngs of our own countrymen – at least these foreigners would impart a vague sense of living abroad. But as it happened the northern Europeans were generally more settled and in consequence their properties rarely came on the market.

Despite the many warnings so eagerly pressed upon us concerning the drawbacks and intrinsic dangers of a more isolated rural location, we remained haughtily aloof from all such kindly advice. We definitely knew better: we wanted the ethnic simplicity and bucolic charm of the real Spain, and blow the consequences. Not for us the neatly whitewashed clusters of identical villas thrown up overnight for the expats in countless sprawling urbanisations, nor the ornately castellated villas set within some exclusive, gated complex. Plant a palm tree, add a couple of arches onto the elevations of a plain bungalow, attach a blue and yellow ceramic nameplate to the gatepost and suddenly it was the Spanish Dream? That might be an enticing prospect for many people, particularly as a holiday home, but it was never going to work for us; any sojourn longer than a weekend in such surroundings would like as not bring despair.

Neither could we ever imagine ourselves fitting in with the compulsory gin and bridge evenings at the nearest golf club, less still with the quiz nights and happy hour banter of the bar flies in search of a better wife at the local English pub. We had been unwittingly lured by well intentioned, if somewhat older friends towards each of these delights during our first weeks in Moraira. The experience had nearly put paid to Spain forever. But the awkwardness cut both ways, for Jani and I were not easily pigeonholed; our relative youth and the footloose manner of our sabbatical seemed to leave us adrift within the hierarchies of the Costa Blanca. (What opprobrium that innocent name can still so unfairly conjure up!)

Jani knew the area well from her Spring term in Jávea with AV, who also happened to be a friend of my parents. More recently Jani and I had visited Spain several times to cement the region in our affections; I had considered many other destinations for our sabbatical, but none had the particular pull that Jani felt for the Marina Alta region. Several acquaintances in the area had been kind enough to allow us a glimpse into their expatriate lives and between them we could pick out what would be important to us; but in truth the only fundamental requirement would be a reasonable proximity to the recently opened international school in Jávea.

Most importantly we wanted a unique property, something with a very specific appeal to set it apart from the hundreds of identical villas flooding the market at any given time. We had visited several hopefuls in a furry of viewings during our first days in Moraira, but all that separated these houses was the variety of mildew spores in the cupboards, or the number of settlement cracks in the walls. Every one of them attested to yet another hasty and very costly exit from Spain, each departure inevitably leaving behind the tangible signs of neglect above a silent undertone of bitter regret.

Then we came across something truly extraordinary: an unfinished villa at the very top of the building line on the high slopes of Montgó. Most attractively designed around a cloistered courtyard, where provision had already been made for a central garden with an ornamental fountain at its centre, it was a gem that had really turned our heads. This 'architect designed' villa – not to be confused with a villa conceived by a chimpanzee, although notable examples of their work abound in alarming profusion – had been built on its own little plateau at a safe distance in front of a sheer wall of rock that rose several hundred feet to the mountain summit. The lie of the land would prevent anything being built beside it or behind it, for fear of the regular rock falls. Beyond its front boundary the land fell away so sharply that none of the many villas already built on the lower slopes were visible; instead the panorama was filled with a lofty view over the farmland in the valley, stretching away eastward to the sea and towards distant mountains to south and west. The architect had made ample use of the local honey coloured stone to set off traditional white elevations within and without. Neither Jani nor I could find fault with its spacious, flowing design. One corner of the inner courtyard abutted the main part of the house, while the farther end led to a casita, a swimming pool and an expanse of terraces with garaging beneath. There was much to marvel at.

We were spellbound, but unfortunately the ticket price for the fully completed villa was every bit as expensive as it looked. Had we been intending to stay in Spain for more than our allotted two years we would have snapped it up there and then, but the reality was very different. After our sojourn in Spain we intended to settle for at least ten years in England, where our children's education would take precedence; for that period in our lives we would need a comfortable home in Devon where they could spend a more settled childhood. As we couldn't afford two lavish homes we reluctantly let this magical villa slip through our fingers, consoling ourselves with the thought of how much money we had saved.

I was beginning to think our sabbatical might have been a colossal mistake, but in the nick of time I chanced upon a brief advertisement in a local newspaper for a simple finca located in the countryside just beyond the sleepy village of Jesús Pobre. Details of the property were scant, but the asking price seemed astonishingly reasonable and Jani wasted no time in persuading me to arrange a viewing for the following morning. Set quietly some eight miles inland above a tranquil valley cultivated with almond and orange trees, the simple one street village boasted a promising looking bakery – fondly remembered by Jani – a less remarkable neon-lit bar and, lurking behind a grimy fly screen, a grocery smaller than a hermit's larder. (The village's famous *riurau*, the attractively arched, open sided building used in former times for drying moscatel grapes into raisins, had not yet been reinvented as a covered market and remained an unused ruin at the time.)

We pressed on between the unremarkable buildings at either side of the village's narrow main street, our English number plate arousing a suspicious twitching of dusty lace curtains in its wake. The tarmac quickly petered out beyond the last few houses, turning into a dirt track as we emerged gratefully onto the flank of a wide valley, where ribbons of frost still lingered at the foot of low stone walls that marked out the many smallholdings. Here and there thin plumes of smoke rose straight into the still air from a dozen unseen chimneys hidden amongst the distant trees, beyond which the snow capped serrations above faraway Guadalest glistened in the sunlight on the high horizon. The prospect beguiled us immediately.

The valley's fields and surrounding hillsides had been meticulously planted over the generations, presenting us with a marshalled patchwork quilt of soft pink almond blossom interspersed with polished green ranks of orange trees, themselves decoratively speckled with glowing globes of ripening fruit amidst their own white mantle of blossom. At the nether end of the valley the rotund stubs of three disused windmills stood like freshly moulded sandcastles on the skyline atop a wooded knoll, below which our destination evidently nestled. Spying the finca in the distance for the first time on that crisp and cloudless January day, no more than a slim triangle of whitewashed gable and a shard of terracotta roof peeping above the glistening groves, the property appeared more than promising. Eagerly we followed the directions, snaking our way down the winding track until we eventually came to a fork in the road next to a spinney of pine and chestnut, thence to a clearing where we drew up beside a tall hedge of oleander. As we climbed out of the car a heavenly wave of perfume from the orange groves washed over us like a silent Atlantic roller.

Waiting to meet us in the courtyard we found a tall, distinguished looking man in his late fifties taking his ease on the low wall surrounding the finca's well. Dressed like Indiana Jones in safari shirt, red and white spotted neckerchief, blue denim jeans and snake boots – less the fedora and rifle slung over one shoulder – Roy reminded me of someone I couldn't quite place, until one of my mother-in-law Audrey's stage whispers (think Town Cryer) soughed forth from the back of our car to jolt my memory.

"Good heavens, Ronnie," she said to Jani's father. "It's Stewart Granger!"

Roy pretended not to hear; I imagine he had heard such a comparison many times before. There was good reason too, although there was not a shred of vanity in him, for he undoubtedly possessed the sickeningly handsome film star looks of any of those post-war screen idols. He and his equally charming wife Gill, who lived on the farther side of the valley when they weren't at home on the Isle of Man, would turn out to be the most charming couple we could ever wish to meet; they would also become valued advisors during our time in Spain and firm friends thereafter. Before we began our tour of the finca Roy explained he was acting on behalf of his brother-in-law, who had spent too many years under the sun and was on doctor's orders to part with his holiday home.

The quaint stone and whitewash finca ran to one sitting room – large enough for several cats to be energetically swung – that was set between an attractive kitchen with traditional latticework cupboards and a party size bathroom most charitably described as retro-skinflint-minimalist. Upstairs two generous bedrooms were blessed with high, vaulted ceilings; one of them opened onto a charming, rough-hewn, covered balcony such as one might see on a postcard of a mountain chalet in Switzerland; the slightly larger of the two overlooked the pool from a perfect little half-lantern, birdcage balcony – an original *reja*, in fact. Rustic clay setts on the ground floor lay in gentle undulations on top of compacted earth beneath, while the bowed ceilings above were lined with gesso between heavy pine rafters. An assortment of heavy chestnut doors, rippled glass fanlights and delicate sections from an ornately carved screen – all reclaimed from a church in Zaragoza – delighted our eyes. No two windows or doors were the same shape, size or style; it was exactly as an old finca should be. More practically a simple open fireplace snuggled in a corner opposite the original dogleg staircase, where well trodden stone steps rose unevenly above a pair of arched bookcases. Most re-assuringly the entire house smelled sweet and there was not a single patch of dampness or woodworm to be seen.

Outside, an extended family of sparrows argued noisily in the plumbago, where fresh growth was already threatening to cover the property's simple, pressed metal nameplate fixed to the stone pillar beside the gate.

Beyond the finca's inner courtyards, shaded *nayas* and un-adorned swimming pool there stood a charming casita that had been similarly restored, its original russet and amber stonework glowing in the low January sun. A slender metal chimney descended from the apex of the raftered ceiling in the main room, its broad hood hovering over a raised fireplace; around this focal point some easy chairs and a dining table were haphazardly arranged away from a simple kitchen and a shower room. One end of the room had been screened off for a pair of beds and in the far corner a raised divan had been built in the Levantine fashion to provide a pair of occasional beds and extra seating. The casita was close enough to the main house and closer still to the swimming pool for convenience, yet secluded enough to provide ideal guest accommodation. The surrounding gardens were shielded by unruly hedges of laurel and other evergreens known collectively in Spanish as *siempreverde*; beyond one of these hedges lay a further area of fallow land large enough to accommodate a tennis court, should the owner be so inclined.

Both these simple, thick-walled farm buildings had been breathed upon a decade earlier by an architect from the Pays d'Oc, whose careful eye had sensitively converted them from bucolic squalour to a hand-painted tile's thickness above spartan discomfort. Several original stone archways were the only features that dispelled an overriding impression of rustic Galician charm, somehow spirited by magic carpet to the Marina Alta. Better still, we learned, the few neighbours in the valley were all Spanish farmers, one of whom gratefully tended the dozens of vines, citrus and olive trees within the finca's one acre boundary in return for the lion's share of produce. Rows of mature moscatel vines behind the house stood lovingly banked up beside furrows of rich soil that had been smoothed solid by repeated cycles of sun and frost. As I stepped out between the gnarled trunks of these immaculately cultivated vines, each one neatly pruned to waist height, the delusive surface of the tilled soil gave way underfoot like the crust of a soft chocolate velvet pie.

Of course the expected profusions of bougainvillea sprang from every corner of the courtyards, ready to grow their welcome summer shade over the pergolas and up every other wall. Maturing agaves towered twenty feet above their younger offspring next to the pool, threatening to burst into majestic flower at any moment before they withered and died away; I was already contemplating how on earth I would dispose of their vast and dangerously prickly remains. Framing the picture behind the valley stood the massive western rump of Montgó, the mammoth-like mountain that dominates the seaboard where it falls away towards the coast and separates the towns of Jávea and Dénia.

Astonishingly this finca, named 'La Abubilla' after the hoopoe bird, could be ours for much less than the cost of our floating gin gazebo and at a fraction of the price of the deplorable villas we had so mistakenly viewed. To his credit Roy had confided that his brother-in-law had experienced 'some occasional trouble with vagrants' at the finca during his long absences in England. A more astute house hunter might have pricked up his ears at this snippet of information, but a surge of uncharacteristic optimism was already washing away any concerns we might otherwise have nursed. More pragmatically the possibility of the most determined vagrant ever breaking into this property seemed utterly implausible to me. Double locks, heavy bolts, chains and iron grilles at every door and window convinced me the place was self-evidently more secure than the Crown Jewels; after all I had spent my childhood in a farmhouse that boasted neither lock nor key to its front door.

Our reply to the advertisement had been the very first response; since then Roy and Gill's telephone had been ringing itself off the hook; viewings by other interested parties had already been arranged later in the day. Acting with unaccustomed haste Jani and I mulled over the conflict between *gift horse* and *too good to be true* for all of ten seconds before offering the full asking price. A typically Mediterranean bargain – neatly split between cash and declared value – was immediately struck and the formalities completed within days. Three weeks later a few sticks of suitable furniture were delivered from storage in Sussex, and with their arrival our Spanish sabbatical had properly begun.

La Abubilla, we soon discovered, had not been inhabited for quite some time. As a holiday home it had seldom been occupied for more than a month or so in summer, and more rarely still during the winter months. Idleness, as any mechanic, physiotherapist or neurologist will tell you, can be far more deleterious than over-exertion; and so it proved with our electricity supply. The curse of Jani's hairdryer soon struck again, the brute refusing to work on its lowest setting without plunging the house into darkness. A man from the electricity board's emergency service had attended in double-quick time (less than a fortnight after we had called him) but he could only suggest we paid to upgrade the overhead power lines from the village at a cost of three million pesetas. This was a depressing prospect of the sort we had so often been warned to expect in the countryside. But when the power began to fuse every time six feeble lightbulbs were switched on at the same time, I decided to investigate the problem myself before shelling out such a large sum of money. Armed with thick rubber gloves, an insulated screwdriver and a rubber mat from Miranda's baby bath on which to stand, I stripped back the live supply cables and clamped freshly exposed copper wire into the junction box. Hey presto! We could turn on every single light in the house at the same time as the toaster, the kettle and the swimming pool pump. Even Jani's hairdryer could be turned on full bore without causing a major power outage in Jesús Pobre; better still, the monster heated up the entire house within seconds on frosty mornings. My foolhardy remedy had cost precisely nothing, although I wouldn't advise anyone attempt it without hefty life insurance. Jani claimed my remedy was exactly what she would have suggested and wanted to know why on earth I hadn't thought of it before.

Contrary to all pessimistic expectation, a new bath, two fridges and an immersion heater were all we required to civilise the finca. Outside, the narrow terraces beside the pool would benefit from extension with a surrounding balustrade for the children's safety, but that was the sum of our expenses. (Some time after we had moved in I also gave Miguel the gardener a handsome reward for supplying us with a bucket of live eels: they were necessary, he had insisted, to purify the water in our well, which we drew by hand whenever the mains supply failed.) But all in all Jani and I had got away extremely lightly considering we had bought our finca in such haste, and without the slightest thought of a survey.

In fact our car was causing us far more trouble than anything else. Built by British Leyland, albeit at the higher end of their range of miserable vehicles, it took an instant dislike to life in a warmer climate. Its fuel system threw the spanners out of the

Hoopoes   © *Jani Tully Chaplin*

toolbox every time the afternoon sun warmed the March air above twenty-five degrees; the air conditioning only whimpered into life when there was a frost on the ground and the electric windows obstinately refused to close when a sudden shower came by. Worse still its distinctive yellow English number plate and right hand steering wheel had a hypnotic effect on the Spanish traffic police, particularly when they had fallen short of their daily quota of fines. Seemingly they were subconsciously drawn to our car like moths to a candle. We could park in a row of Spanish cars and be the only one to receive a ticket; we could drive through a village in a steady stream of traffic and be singled out like a black sheep for a speeding fine.

Trickle slowly from a slip road onto a carriageway bereft of any traffic for a mile in either direction, as all Spanish drivers regularly did with impunity on their way to Jávea, and ours would be the one car to be picked on. A police motorcyclist would roar up from nowhere and fine me 25,000 pesetas, cash on the spot, for failing to come to a complete halt at the white line. It was easy money and I began to suspect I was being stalked. Only after my third infringement did I notice how this vindictive love child of Robocop and Easy Rider had taken up permanent residence on a flyover a little way down the road, whence he could easily spy our yellow number plate. No paperwork was ever issued for each fine, but I knew further consequences would likely follow if I asked for a receipt from this sinister, leather-clad, Ray-Ban wearing hoodlum. The rogue must have retired to Cuba or the Argentine long ago, and to this day I still feel a warm glow of gratification as I remember how much I was able to contribute so generously to his pension fund. These annoyances stopped as soon as we bought a new Renault seven seater, its white Spanish number plate and white livery amply demonstrating we had joined the ranks of more sensible Spaniards. For extra authenticity the shiny new car was soon defaced with *Disponible tambien en blanco,* (also available in white), scrawled by some wag in the accumulated layers of ochre dust on its tailgate.

My parents were very critical of our new car when they had come to visit us and considered it a great extravagance, although they were pleased enough to be driven around the Costa Blanca in spacious comfort. Liz had refused to drive with Michael after their tempestuous journey through France and was threatening to fly home when the time came to leave Spain; there had, she confided, been too many close shaves and heart stopping 'where did he come from!' moments that had frayed her nerves beyond endurance. However an altogether more serious worry began to play on my mind following a quite extraordinary sequence of events that unfolded during my parents' time with us at La Abubilla.

Liz and Michael had been invited to spend a couple of nights with some old friends of the family who were building a grand house high above the Jalon Valley, a few miles further inland from us. Perhaps fifteen years younger than my parents they were affluent and fearfully glamorous – Henrietta having been a Dior model and Guy a highly successful businessman. Guy had just been proposed as a DL when the pair had upped sticks and moved to Spain; I knew things had not gone too swimmingly for them since the move, but I had no idea quite how badly until my mother related the strange circumstances of their brief stay. The moment my parents arrived at the finished wing of the new house Guy had demanded their passports, bank cards, cash and any jewellery they might be carrying. These valuables were immediately locked in an impressive safe hidden behind a fridge in the kitchen. Even more bizarrely Henrietta confessed that her larder was utterly bare; but its was Guy's insistence they should remain indoors at all times, owing to an expected plague of hornets, that was so questionable.

This peculiar behaviour had greatly alarmed my parents, as did their hosts' habit of peeping nervously through the shutters every other minute. In the morning after a breakfast of black coffee and dry cheese crackers Guy and Henrietta announced they needed to make an urgent visit to their bank in Dénia. My mother insisted she accompany them, hoping for an opportunity to buy some provisions for their lunch, and Guy reluctantly agreed. Half-an-hour later Guy's highly conspicuous, canary yellow Mercedes drew up directly outside the bank, whereupon he instructed his wife to move over to the driver's seat and keep the engine running. Well, you can imagine what my mother made of that. After a tense fifteen minutes Guy walked briskly out of the bank carrying a battered Gladstone bag and dived into the car shouting '*Go, Hen*! *Drive!*' before he had even closed the passenger door. Off they sped as their eyes barely left the rear-view mirrors, although no wailing sirens or flashing blue lights had followed the car.

Nothing more was said until they were once again safely locked inside their villa, when the couple meekly confessed they had become caught up in a bitter ransom strip dispute. The conflict had been deliberately engineered by some very unsavoury English characters, who had been known to resort to violence. By no means the first such fraudulent claim in the area, Henrietta explained, the swindle could only have been perpetrated with the connivance of a corrupt notary and a willing accomplice at the land registry office; as such the deception would be virtually impossible to disprove. The morning's escapade had involved a fruitful attempt by Guy to 'borrow' some crucial files from the bank before the English rogues could successfully close off all access and rights of way to the new villa. Without legal access to their land, their villa would be worthless and would need to be demolished unless they paid an exorbitant ramsom. Guy and Henrietta were plainly terrified.

How, my mother asked me when she returned to our finca the following day, had two such upstanding people been brought so low? They were well connected county socialites, living until a year ago in a Cotswold manor house; they stood on prestigious committees, for heaven's sake! The whole thing sounded too absurd for words, although Michael emerged from his silence to voice his uncharitable opinion that people who sailed too close to the wind deserved whatever they got. Some months later Jani and I happened to be driving through the Jalon Valley and called in to check on Henrietta and Guy, only to find their villa entirely empty. Nothing more was heard from them until the following Christmas, when a card bearing no return address arrived out of the blue from Italy; an enclosed note apologetically explained how they had been forced to flee Spain in a great hurry soon after my parents had visited. We never heard from them again. This incident remained an unsettling mystery I could well have done without, given that precise details of the boundaries shown on our own finca's title deeds were about as well defined and permanent as a trail of feathers in a hurricane.

Chapter 6 – Jani
Follow The Yellow Brick Road...

Toto, I've a feeling we're not in Kansas anymore.

The Wonderful Wizard of Oz
L. Frank Baum

Great excitement ensued during the next few days as Rory's birthday approached at the beginning of April. As all mothers will remember, parties for young children had to be planned well in advance, so before term ended at the Lady Elizabeth School I had handed party invitations to each child in Rory's class. No responses came, accepting or otherwise, despite our telephone number and RSVP being clearly printed on the bottom of the cards. This was all rather worrying, having no way of contacting the parents since none of them actually had telephones. In these days of mobile phones, emails and social media the disadvantages of isolation may seem hard to grasp for people who have never had to write a proper letter, or, in the direst of emergencies, send a telegram. I had no addresses for the parents and, even if I had, the Spanish postal system was spasmodic, slow and, when fiestas and football matches intervened, entirely inoperative. I tried to reassure Jeremy and Liz that everyone would turn up on the day, although I was secretly worried I had made a dreadful error of judgement; obviously I should have asked each of the parents if they would be bringing their children to the party before the end of term. I had booked a children's entertainer from Benidorm and had shopped for party food, balloons, paper bunting, party bags with the little novelties and sweets to fill them, and prizes for the games. Luckily most of the tiny shops in the narrow streets of Jávea Old Town were crammed with such things, fiestas being high on every Spaniard's agenda. Every other week there was a feast day and celebration somewhere in Spain; Rory rather confusingly called them 'Siestas'.

I paid a visit to the renowned bakery where we bought our bread each day and asked them to make a large sponge cake, intending to decorate it myself. They spoke not a word of English and, as it would be a surprise, I couldn't use Rory as interpreter. The bakery made delicious little sponge cakes flavoured with orange flower water, so in my best Spanish I tried to explain that I would like a giant version of these *Magdalenas*. The rotund lady who served in the shop seemed to be doing her level best not to understand me and kept adding more and more little cakes to the one I had picked from the counter to demonstrate. In the end, after about ten minutes of misunderstanding, I resorted to drawing a sketch of a large cake on one of her paper napkins and indicated the size required with both hands held apart at a distance of about eighteen inches. Thankfully the peseta dropped and she nodded and smiled. When did I need the cake, she asked. I said I would collect it on the first day of April and hoped they didn't have our tradition of April Fools' Day. When I told Jeremy and Liz how difficult this task had been, they were pessimistic and worried that the cake would never materialise. But there was no choice; I had no baking tins, our ancient little oven was a law unto itself and there were power cuts every other day that would easily ruin a half baked cake. If I had planned things better and had a large tin, I could have driven over to the marina and baked the cake in Seahawk's oven, which was far superior – as was the galley.

I collected the cake from the bakery in good time and I was immensely relieved to see it was waiting for me on the counter, round, golden, splendidly wrapped in cellophane and absolutely perfect. I smuggled it back into the house while Rory, Jeremy and Liz were busy hanging balloons and paper decorations around the naya where the party would be held. As soon as the children were in bed that evening I began to decorate the giant cake. Rory's favourite cartoon character at the time was the *Pink Panther,* so I made a vast quantity of bright pink icing and carved the sponge cake into a panther head shape. With trembling fingers and the largest bread knife I could find, I very carefully sliced the cake horizontally through the middle and spread a thick layer of strawberry jam to sandwich the two halves together. So far so good. The pink icing went on smoothly and when it had dried sufficiently I used black food colouring and a small watercolour brush to paint the panther face details and the whole effect was perfect. But then I realised I had no tin big enough to hold the cake and I couldn't leave it out in the kitchen, for we were plagued with an army of minute sugar obsessed ants that found their way into every cupboard and drawer, despite regular dosings with peppermint oil. As the fridges were already full of party food, Jeremy came up with the brilliant suggestion to put the cake in the oven where neither Rory nor the resident ants would find it. We went to bed very pleased with ourselves, yet still worried if any guests would turn up for the party. The next morning dawned sunny and warm and Jeremy left me in bed feeding Miranda while he went downstairs to make tea.

"I've turned the oven on for the croissants." he said proudly as he returned with two steaming mugs of Earl Grey.

"THE CAKE!" I shrieked, as baby Miranda jumped out of her

skin and off my bosom and Jeremy spilt his tea.

He leapt down the stone staircase two at a time, rescuing the Pink Panther from the oven just in time, although beads of moisture were already glistening on the strawberry pink icing. Eventually we managed to find and clean out an old plastic washing tub to cover the cake and hide it from Rory until it was needed.

The garden and naya looked very festive and colourful with a host of decorations. Chairs were placed in the courtyard facing the naya where the entertainer would perform, I spread some rugs on the paving stones for the invited children and set out every chair we possessed in case any parents chose to stay for the party. As soon as lunch was finished Rory ran to the drive to watch for the first cars to snake their way through the orange groves on their way to our house. With immaculate timing Liz asked me what on earth we were going to do if nobody turned up. I had no answer, but we all realised what a crushing disappointment it would be for Rory if the party was only attended by his small family of five.

"Mummy! Come quickly, I can see someone coming!" Rory called from the drive. We all raced to the drive but the car that pulled up was only a small van driven by the magician from Benidorm. We showed him into the garden and he set up his paraphernalia in front of the naya as Rory ran back to the drive. The next hour was the longest I can ever remember, an agony of anxiously peering up the sleeping valley every five minutes to see if anyone would be bothered to come, or if everyone else was officially on SPT, Spanish Procrastination Time. Shortly after the party was due to start, we heard another yell from Rory.

"Look! They're coming!"

Breathing deep sighs of relief we all peered towards the lane where a stream of cars were snaking, nose to tail in a convoy, down the hill towards us. Each little guest and their parents were welcomed with hugs and kisses and we were surprised that along with gaily wrapped presents, most of the mothers had also turned up with all their other children, explaining that children's parties were such a rarity in that part of Spain that they hoped we wouldn't mind if they joined in too. We wouldn't have cared if they had brought the entire Spanish Army, so relieved were we that Rory would have so many guests for his sixth birthday party. Dressed in their best party frocks, the little girls sat on the chairs, Adam and some of the older brothers sat or stood behind them and a few mothers joined us on the remaining chairs. The magician gave a wonderful performance and had probably the most enthusiastic and appreciative audience he had ever entertained.

Liz and Jeremy helped me carry the party food to the shaded naya where we had laid the table with paper cloths, colourful napkins and plates. Jeremy poured glasses of wine for the grown ups and lemonade, apple or orange juice for the children. Liz had made delicate finger sandwiches with various fillings – cucumber, Marmite, egg mayonnaise and tuna. I had added cocktail sausages on sticks and a couple of cheese and pineapple 'hedgehogs', a great favourite with most of the children I knew. To make the food go further for our extra guests, we rapidly opened every packet of snacks in the cupboards and filled all the bowls we had. "*Compleaños feliz!*" sang the children as I brought the cake out of the kitchen and Rory was thrilled to see the Pink Panther as he blew out the six candles. One of the English mothers kindly stayed on after the other guests had left to help clear up, while her pretty little daughter was rowed around the swimming pool by

Rory in his inflatable boat; it was a scene straight from *Swallows and Amazons* – Spanish style. There were some sandwiches left over and our helper asked if she could eat them as she adored Marmite sandwiches; Liz immediately nicknamed her 'Mrs. Marmite', which she was affectionately called from that day on; I still can't recall her real name but I do remember she and her husband ran a very successful business exporting Iceberg lettuce to British supermarkets.

Having entirely ignored the celebrations Michael emerged gloomily from his sanctuary in the casita, as soon as he thought the coast was clear, to ask when his supper was going to be served. Utterly unbelievable. That apart, a potentially disastrous day had turned into the best children's party ever for Rory and a birthday none of us will easily forget.

As Spring gave up its cooler winds and the last blossom fell from the trees, we awoke one dawn to find summer had crept in while we slept; light sweaters and trousers were replaced with tee-shirts and shorts, Rory happily discarding his ski boots and opting for flip-flops. One morning after Jeremy had left to take Rory to school, I decided the chore of ironing would be far more agreeably completed outside in the garden. Miranda was taking her morning nap, so I parked her pram beside my ironing board in the shade of our solitary date palm, the soft whispering of its fronds in the gentle breeze disturbed only by the indistinct strains of classical music coming from my transistor radio in the kitchen. Just as I became entirely lost in thought, I heard a familiar voice in the front courtyard.

"Hello the house!" called Roy as he walked up to the pool with his faithful Alsatian.

Finding me there alone with Miranda he asked where Jeremy was. Roy looked highly alarmed when I told him.

"Jani. Please don't venture outside when Jeremy isn't here, especially with Miranda," he warned. "Always stay in the house, lock all the doors and never leave your radio switched on."

I asked why but Roy was vague, simply inferring it was generally safer – safer from what precisely he wouldn't say. My offer of coffee was politely refused; after helping me into the house with my ironing board and Miranda's pram, he reminded me to lock all the doors, leaving before Jeremy returned. I should have been more suspicious, but the advice was soon forgotten ... until our next guests came to stay.

Our old friends from South Devon, Tim, Din and their three year-old son James were the easygoing sort of companions we could relax with anywhere. For their first evening in Spain we decided the seven of us would drive into neighbouring Dénia for supper. The restaurant we had chosen, set in a cool inner courtyard filled with tubs of potted plants surrounding a central fountain, was situated in a secluded lane that led off one of the town's beautiful, tree lined streets. We grown ups enjoyed a favourite starter of green Padrón peppers fried in olive oil and sprinkled with coarse sea salt crystals; they were pretty fiery but the dish was always accompanied by a dry, ice cold white wine, poured into short stemmed china goblets slightly bigger than saké cups. The delicious wine only soothed the heat of the peppers for a few blissful moments before the fire on our palates flared up again with a vengeance. Neither water nor beer had the slightest remedial effect, so, much against our will we were obliged to consume substantial quantities of the medicinal wine to prevent permanent damage to our taste buds.

It was pitch dark downstairs when we arrived home at La Abubilla in very jolly mood and invited our friends to come in for a nightcap before they turned in at the casita. Long before Jeremy found the light switch we could already hear the unwelcome sound of broken glass underfoot; then, to our horror, as the glow of a table lamp revealed upturned furniture and ornaments scattered over the floor, we noticed the French windows at the far side of the room hanging open, their glazing shattered and the protective grills bent apart. A robbery was not exactly the welcoming first night we had planned for our old friends, who remained remarkably unperturbed by the incident as they helped us clear up the worst of the mess before retiring to bed.

Chastened and suddenly very sober, Jeremy and I laid awake for the rest of the night as we wondered whether we could ever again feel safe in our charming finca.

As the evenings grew warmer I would sometimes take the children for walks along the dusty goat tracks and narrow lanes that wound their way through the orange groves past fields of leaf covered vines and ancient olive trees. During the day it became too hot for the children to venture far from the pool and welcome shade of our garden. As soon as we stepped outside the little oasis of La Abubilla, an unseen door opened into another climate. With Miranda in her pushchair and Rory on his shiny red go-kart we constituted a strange spectacle. We rarely saw another soul on these early evening sorties into the surrounding countryside. The narrow tracks were quiet apart from local farmers in their ubiquitous, dilapidated Seat vans, encounters that warranted much manoeuvering of our unorthodox procession into the side of the road to allow them to pass. The backs

The view, the house Jeremy built ... and his helpers

Their first fashion show

Miranda's Christening

'Yames Hunt'

Granny and Grandpa Tully in Benidorm

The villa that got away

Viewing La Abubilla and its casita,
January 1988

Pick your own

Carnivals and fiestas

Superman and water baby

Miranda and Rory keeping busy at sea

Unspoilt Espalmador

*Crowded anchorage at
CalaVedella, Ibiza*

Nativity play

Those purple tracksuits

The morning croissant run

A farewell to Spain from the top of Montgo, 2,500 feet high

Settling into a new home in South Devon

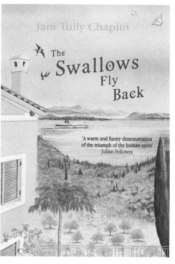

Jani's Corfu Trilogy continues where this book ends and describes her family's fifteen happy and eventful years in the Ionian, living amongst the joyous Corfiots, before a life-changing setback delivers them home to England, where they gradually rebuild their lives in Cornwall.

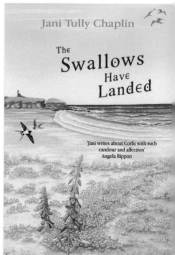

of these vans carried the oddest assortment of cargo; often the rear doors were left open, swinging wildly, and within we could see a young goat or a pig, or a clutch of terrified hens skidding from side to side between a large television set, a fridge or a lawnmower as the van lurched over deep potholes. Once we saw a colossal fibreglass model of a mounted toreador lashed to the back of a van, but unlike its unfortunate animal companions this had been securely fastened with a cat's-cradle of orange twine; it looked like Gulliver pinned to the ground by the Lilliputians. To the west of the valley rose the high sierras, our Elephant Hills, smoky blue in the twilight.

As Rory's legs pedalled furiously, the go-kart swerving all over the road, Miranda thoroughly enjoyed the distraction of his enactment of the Monaco Grand Prix going on ahead of her. Meanwhile I revelled in the chance to study my neighbours' properties more closely. The few humble farmhouses scattered nearby were well away from the track we took by car. Having the children with me justified a very slow amble past these gardens, giving me plenty of time to admire their contents without appearing too inquisitive. Tiny white stars of jasmine, with their deliciously expensive scent, twinkled from their fronds of pointed dark green leaves. Thick swathes of bougainvillea covered every available inch of wall space and hung heavily over wrought iron gates and railings, spilling their vibrant shocks of colour in all directions. Through open doors it was amusing to see how many mopeds and motor bikes lived inside the houses; dogs and cats however were relegated to the garden sheds– such a contrast to England.

One balmy evening we met Miguel shuffling along the road on his way home from the fields. His tortured gait was the product of a lifetime spent hunched over the squat vines, only moving a foot at a time from one plant to the next; it had been a shock to learn he had only seen fifty-two summers. Dressed in his usual outfit of faded French blue, he stood to one side to let us to pass and swept off his tattered straw hat in a very cavalier gesture. Clutching it to his stomach he gruffly croaked a formal '*Buenos tardes Señora*', his throat obviously in need of refreshment after the day's labour. I made my customary attempt at polite conversation but noticed as I was talking that his eyes, twinkling like a hedgehog's in his leathery brown face, were firmly fixed on the go-kart. As a boy, had he perhaps dreamed of owning such a vehicle?

I tried to imagine how very different Miguel's childhood must have been from Rory's; this fellow, whose toil had aged him far beyond his years, who knew nothing of the delights of Hamleys, of West End musicals, of careering around a warmly carpeted house in a diminutive Superman costume, or of carefree holidays on faraway beaches and snow covered mountains. Miguel had worked his parcels of land for little reward, like generations before him; the extent of his world reached little further than the horizons visible from the peak of Montgó, or to the squiggly black and white images on the temperamental television set in the local bar. My range of Spanish pleasantries finally exhausted, we exchanged a final, 'Hasta luego'. Miguel's eyes were still admiring the go-kart wistfully as Rory sat on the grid of another imaginary Grand Prix, revving furiously from the depths of his throat. Miguel stood motionless, following our progress with rapt attention. Suddenly, and with an unexpected worldliness, he called a cheery 'Yames Hunt!' after us. Rory beamed back at him over his shoulder, swelling with pride as he clattered off along the road.

Rory came back from school one day at the start of the summer term with the exciting news that the Lady Elizabeth would be putting on a musical show at the theatre in Jávea at the end of term. All 60 pupils would take part in *The Wizard of Oz* and Rory was looking forward to the whole thing immensely, knowing all the songs already from watching the video of the famous Judy Garland film many times. Rory had the theatre in his blood, both grandmothers having been dancers in their youth. Readers of my Corfu Trilogy will remember that Jeremy's mother was a principal ballerina with Ballet Rambert, with whom she had toured the world. My mother had been an enthusiastic member of the Torquay Dramatic and Operatic Society, acting, dancing and singing in many pre-war productions at The Pavilion.

Next morning when I took Rory to school, his teacher asked me if I would be willing to restore the head of the Pantomime horse they wanted to include in the show. Evidently someone had told her that I did a bit of painting. Of course I willingly agreed but was rather startled to see the head size of this monster horse. It was loaded onto the front seat of my car and secured with the seat belt, staring with hollow sightless eyes through the windscreen and getting many double takes from other motorists in return. All the way back home I kept wondering where a pantomime horse could appear in The Wizard of Oz. Was that horrific scene in *The Godfather* going to be spliced into the script? Then I remembered the Horse of a Different Colour and breathed a sigh of relief.

Bearing this in mind I set to work in the sunny courtyard with the enormous head propped on the garden table; it was made out of papier maché but was still heavy and I pitied whoever had to wear it. I used my gouache paints to give a pastel rainbow of colour as a background, then worked on the face with sparkly nail varnish and bright blue eye shadow and sprayed glitter on the white nylon mane and forelock. I made some outsize false eyelashes by cutting shiny black paper into fringes and sticking them on the top and bottom of the eye shaped holes. Jeremy said it looked more like a Jersey cow than a horse but Rory was delighted with it and so was the school. I thought my contribution to the show was complete, until I was asked if I would help with the make-up for the principal characters, as the producer of the show obviously thought I had a flair for such things. I walked straight into that one!

By this time we had become good friends with Lynda and Ian, the English parents of three year-old Carmella who was in the reception class at the Lady Elizabeth, having first met them all at one of Gill's lunch parties; they lived in a luxurious villa, about five times the size of our finca on the lower slopes of Montgó. Gill had wanted to introduce us to people of our own age and had arranged the lunch especially for our benefit. With typical thoughtfulness she realised Rory and Carmella might need a bit of entertaining while the grown ups chatted, so she created a treasure hunt for them; simple clues were left around the villa and garden, written on pieces of paper that Rory helped Carmella to read. It kept both children happily occupied for about an hour, eventually they found their treasure and ran to show us. Each child held a small red box and inside was a beautifully hand made tiny grey furry rabbit, Rory's dressed in boys' clothes and Carmella's in a dress; I still have Rory's to this day. Gill told us she had made the little rabbits herself before raiding Roy's very tidy workshop for the boxes in which he had kept small nails and screws.

Lynda had also been asked to help with the make up, much to my relief; between the two of us we could easily manage the make up for Dorothy, the Scarecrow, the Cowardly Lion, the Tin Man, two Witches and the Wizard – three and a half actors each would be a doddle. Rory and his friend Adam were to be foxes in a scene where the girls in their class would be rabbits and they would perform to *Bright Eyes*, the theme music from *Watership Down*, although how exactly that fitted in to the Wizard of Oz I dreaded to think. In late June the day of the show dawned sunny and hot, even at eight in the morning when I dropped Rory at school the heat was intense. It was going to be blistering hot in the old un-air conditioned theatre, the show being a matinée performance; curtain up would be precisely when the sun was at its zenith. Jeremy looked after Miranda in the foyer as Lynda and I disappeared through the stage door, armed with boxes of cheap and cheerful make-up from the local shops. A long and narrow, dimly lit corridor stretched ahead of us. One of the teachers squeezed past us with an armful of costumes.

"Where would you like us to do the make-up?" I asked, hopeful of a nice large dressing room with decent lighting.

"Oh just here will be fine," she answered. "There's nowhere else!"

Lynda and I looked at each other in horror. How could we survive the stifling, airless corridor for the hour it would take to do the make up for the actors?

"We'll just have to work fast," said Lynda. "At least there are only seven to do!"

Famous last words. We worked our way through the principals, but when it came to the Tin Man we had to combine our skills as so much silver grease paint was involved; we ended up with as much paint on us as on the actor. We were just breathing a sigh of relief having finished in good time, when the chattering and giggling of overexcited children echoed down the corridor from the stage door. The group surged towards us like a tidal wave and came to a halt in front of us, a sea of eager little faces grinning expectantly.

"Hello," I said. "What are you all doing here?"

"We've come to have our make-up done," a small girl answered, cheerfully beaming up at me. "We're in the play."

Lynda and I looked at each other in a complete panic – before us stood twenty-five tiny Munchkins, all desperately longing to have their faces painted.

Mail, unlike in England, was a cause for some excitement. The sound of José Cartero's (Joseph the Postman's) antiquated moped buzzing down the twisting road like an angry hornet sent us all racing for the courtyard as we jostled to be the lucky one to get our hands on the letters. He rarely got as far as our post box, a little wooden affair propped against the well, without being intercepted. It might well have been an ambition of his to actually post the mail into our box; I'm certain I had noticed him creeping into our drive clutching the letters and looking shiftily around for signs of life from the house or garden. However the scrunching of his tattered black boots on the gravel always gave him away. Miranda had an almost sixth sense of anyone approaching; usually in her high chair at breakfast when José arrived, she would swivel herself around to face the door at the first sound.

The joy of receiving our mail owed much to its content – pretty postcards from friends in other parts of the world, or descriptive letters in flimsy blue air mail envelopes from my mother or my aunt in Australia. Mummy's were my favourite as they were always at least five or six pages long, written on both sides and full of news from home, mostly about family and friends, but also keeping me up to date on the state of her roses, the latest Easterly gales and whatever delicacies were flourishing in the vegetable garden. There was never any junk mail and rarely a bill, since most went directly to our bank. For Rory the greatest thrill was to find one of his beloved Granny's parcels. José must have been secretly delighted when he had one of these to deliver as they were too bulky to fit into our post box and he had the pleasure of seeing five year-old Rory's gappy-toothed grin and hearing his lisping '*Grathias*' as it was handed over.

Carefully wrapped in reams of brown paper and secured with layers of Sellotape, finished with string and Grandpa's meticulous knotting, these parcels contained such items we could not find on the Costa Blanca. To a small boy the two tubs of strawberry Nesquick were manna from heaven; to us of course it was Marmite and Earl Grey tea. For some reason talcum powder of any denomination, even Johnsons, was unheard of in Spain, the Señoras seemed to prefer using Agua de Cologna – although the thought of this on baby's bottom made me wince. Having made the decision to live in Spain, we started out with extremely good intentions about entering fully into the experience, only buying local produce, cooking the national dishes, learning the language and customs and immersing ourselves into village life. Some things, however, we found we just could not live without, so Mummy's parcels kept coming.

A formal invitation in Spain was rarer than a Valentine card from the Inland Revenue, so when a 'stiffie' arrived with the post one morning we scrambled to open it. To our great surprise the expensive envelope contained an invitation printed on thick card with gilt edging and a golden palm tree in one corner: our presence was requested at a *Son et Lumière* to be held at a villa somewhere behind Dénia. Lest anyone was baffled, the card helpfully explained that guests would be treated to an evening's entertainment with sound and light. The whole thing sounded splendid as we gaily imagined a highbrow affair featuring a thoughtfully woven historical tableau, themed perhaps on the Moorish invasions of the Iberian peninsula, or even a fanciful pageant based on the Roman settlements in Alicante, and gratefully we accepted. Dress code on the invitation was ambiguous, simply advising 'Smart'. To my fashion guru husband this meant linen trousers, a shirt with a collar and his best pair of Docksides (rather than the pair spattered with antifouling that he usually wore). To some on the Costa Blanca it would undoubtedly prompt the donning of an elaborate 70's-style velvet dinner jacket, probably in maroon, paired with frilled evening shirt, satin bow tie, matching cummerbund and black patent shoes; others might have favoured shorts and a t-shirt that had been washed less than a week ago, (I got that one right). We had arranged for a babysitter to stay with Rory and Miranda for the evening, a competent sixteen year-old pupil of the school. Rory wasn't overly keen on babysitters, but he was delighted to see she was none other than Dorothy from the Wizard of Oz.

The English owners of the villa, our hosts, were prospective parents at the Lady Elizabeth – their children being too young to enrol until the following year – so we had never met either of them until that evening. Directions to the villa led us though an insalubrious area of shabby houses and workshops, so it was quite a surprise to arrive abruptly at the grand gates of a stupendous, wildly elaborate villa. Our fellow guests' cars had spilled out onto the road by the time we had found the house and arrived impolitely late, but for some unknown reason a uniformed flunkey singled us out and directed us to a parking space beside the steps to the portico. Full of gleaming reproduction statuary, this was a property that clearly wouldn't have looked amiss amongst the homes of the rich and famous in Bel-Air. The majority of the Lady Elizabeth parents we had come to know, besides Mrs Marmite and her husband, lived in far more modest houses or apartments – as we certainly did. Many of them, who were striving so valiantly to fund their new lives in the sun by running estate agencies, video rental shops and cocktail bars, or perhaps by working as builders, caretakers and hairdressers, must have wondered where on earth they had come to. Our friends Lynda and Ian, who lived in a very splendid villa, appeared to be the only other parents like ourselves who were fortunate enough to earn an income outside Spain.

Jeremy and I immediately began to wonder who the dickens our hosts were and what they did for a living. And why was this extraordinary miniature palace hidden away behind high walls, and with no views, amidst such a squalid neighbourhood? It all seemed rather curious. Logical connection was all too easily made to colourful rumours circulating about local English gangsters involved in the infamous Brink's-Mat robbery in 1983, when three tons of gold bullion had been stolen. Certainly, we mused, the Spanish Costas had long since acquired an unenviable reputation for harbouring villainous racketeers. Could our host even be one of the gang responsible for hounding our friends Guy and Henrietta out of Spain? Surely not. We were being far too sniffy about the couple who had so kindly invited us to their delightful son et lumière; after all, we naïvely reassured each other, *they* intended to send their two small children to the same school as Rory – an aspiration that was never fulfilled, in the event. Then Jeremy suddenly remembered another moment of similarly assumed, yet thoroughly misplaced trust, when his great aunt had come to stay at the farm in the summer of 1963, when he was fourteen. She was an elderly sugarplum fairy of a maiden aunt, an affectionate, dangerously innocent throwback to a gentler era, who was still in mourning for the death of her betrothed in Flanders almost fifty years earlier. 'I met such a nice man on my train down from Hove,' began Auntie, who invariably met such a nice man on every train journey. 'From Essex I believe, but he was most courteous nonetheless,' she continued. 'Apparently he had just come into a great deal of money and was looking for a quiet place to settle in Torquay.' Jeremy had immediately suggested her nice man sounded suspiciously like one of the Great Train Robbers, all of whom happened to be on the run from the police at the time. 'Good Heavens no, my poppet,' Auntie had replied, steadfast in the immutability of the old order. '*They* wouldn't be travelling first class!'

Beyond the portico we were effusively greeted by our blousey hostess, who had unaccountably mistaken Jeremy for a long lost colleague of her husband. He would be so pleased to see his old friend after all this time, she gushed, as she led us through a cavernous galleried hall, where a circular balcony at its centre overlooked a marble clad indoor swimming pool many feet below us. Shrieks of laughter and much energetic splashing ascended from the grotto amidst a miasma of chlorine; peering over the balcony we could see a group of adults cavorting in the water, some of them still fully dressed and others less so. It was obvious where this particular evening was headed. Following the chatter of strained bonhomie Jeremy and I joined the gathering in the gardens, where our hostess introduced us to several other slightly bewildered guests. Much to our relief her husband was in a conspiratorial huddle with a couple of men the size of gorillas; seeing this entanglement at the farther side of the lawns, where an artificial waterfall cascaded pleasingly into an unseen hollow at the base of a rockery, the dutiful wife firmly steered us away and any embarrassment about our mistaken identity was spared.

An array of plastic tables and chairs had been hired for the occasion and we were invited to find a seat on the extensive terraces surrounding the ostentatiously elaborate outdoor pool, where drinks and canapés were served by buxom young waitresses very obviously dressed by the local costume hire shop – rather inappropriately, I thought – as saucy French maids. As darkness fell, which can happen very abruptly in the Mediterranean, our tuxedo-clad host appeared behind the control desk, adjusted his preposterous wig, which had become precariously animated in the flukey evening breeze, and took to the microphone of his Glastonbury Festival sized sound system.

"Welcome to my sonnett loomyear!" boomed the loudspeakers, immediately launching into the theme from *Star Wars*.

The painfully familiar music was interrupted at intervals by a running commentary from our host beneath the wig, urging his audience's gaze towards a particular palm tree which was then illuminated by a coloured spotlight. As the track came to its climactic end, the whole process was repeated with another tune and the next target to be bathed in colour; luckily for the host, but less fortunately for us, there were many palm trees and other features around the gardens from which to choose. A waterfall turned orange; the ornate bridge over the pool was picked out in lime green; a plaster Venus de Milo was shown to disadvantage in turquoise ... and on it went. It was not long before Jeremy began whispering unflattering comments in my ear to set me giggling.

"I can't sit through much more of this!" Jeremy eventually complained after fifteen long minutes, as Tom Jones wailed forth and the cascade turned bright pink. "Let's go now, nobody will notice."

I was bored too, but after a few glasses of the brandy-laced Sangria I began to feel rather more relaxed than my husband, whose dose of anaesthetic was strictly limited by his imminent driving duties.

"Let's see what the next song is," I replied, without much conviction. "It can only get better."

At that very moment *Will You Miss Me Tonight?*, crooned by Elvis Presley, assailed us at a million decibels and the oleander beside us turned purple. Jeremy was off his seat in a flash, dragging me by the hand and waving a hasty goodbye over his shoulder towards the low flying bosoms and the unfaithful toupée.

"I must just pop to the loo before we drive home," I said as we fled away through the house towards the door, asking a passing French maid for directions to the nearest bathroom.

If I had been astounded by such a profusion of white marble in the galleried hall – flanked with reproduction Doric columns and busts of Greek deities, every one adorned with extravagant floral arrangements of the sort found in ostentatious hotel lobbies worldwide – the bathroom quite took my breath away. Decorated in the Romanesque style, three steps led to a raised platform into which a monstrous black marble bath was sunk. Fake leopardskin rugs, gold plated dolphin taps, wall to ceiling dark tinted mirrors and faux jade accessories completed the Hollywood film set ambience – Cleopatra would have loved it. I found myself unexpectedly looking forward to seeing our own plain and simple bathroom again.

To cap it all, as I made my way out to the portico where Jeremy was waiting for me, I was accosted by a man well into his fifties and well into his tenth pint of sangria. His nose glowing red and his face shiny with perspiration, he pinned me against the wall and slurred his chat-up repartee straight into my face; the seedy womaniser was so close I could smell the alcohol and the last canapé on his breath as I looked helplessly around for a way to escape. I shuffled along as far as I could, until my back was in a corner and I became trapped. Seeing his chance, the leathery roué leant drunkenly towards me, tilted glass in hand dripping deep red sangria onto the white marble floor. Then before he could press home his advantage Jeremy reappeared, wearing his sternest 'unhand my wife' expression and took my arm, gently but firmly leading me outside so fast that I had to trot to keep up with him.

"You attract that sort of man like bees to a honeypot!" exclaimed my husband as soon as we were safely in the car. I wasn't quite sure whether to take this as a compliment or an insult.

* * *

With the arrival of much hotter weather, the towns and villages of the Costa Blanca were preparing themselves for the season of fiestas. During the first week of January the biggest fiesta had been the arrival of the Three Kings, who traditionally made their entrance by boat; but in early summer the narrow streets, where the pretty whitewashed houses were only a few feet away from their neighbours opposite, were completely festooned with canopies of gaily coloured paper decorations; beneath, and not not be outshone, each doorway was embellished with tubs of flowers and small lemon trees. One street in Jávea was decorated on the theme of oranges, with artificial fruits hanging in abundance from the bunting. The small shops at either side were taken over with fancy dress costumes, balloons, fireworks and cellophane packets of luridly coloured sweets – all to be thrown to children from the various carnival floats and horse drawn carriages, or from the riders of stunning Andalusian horses with beautifully Flamenco-costumed ladies seated side saddle behind their elegant gentlemen.

The open air markets were full of colour too – every conceivable fruit and vegetable was artistically arranged and displayed on trestle tables under canvas awnings. A multitude of different olives, glossy with fragrant oil, sat in huge bowls of local pottery; fragrant dried herbs filled the air with their scent and toys to tempt every child swung in the breeze from strings attached to the awnings. One Saturday morning as I was looking at handbags, Rory asked me if I were to buy a leather purse, what colour I would choose. Unsuspectingly I told him, then watched over my shoulder as he went to a stall opposite. Returning to me a minute later, he handed me a tiny red purse he had bought with his pocket money; I still treasure it to this day. Cheap shoes and clothes, (including the biggest pairs of ladies' pants I have ever seen), handbags, belts, towels and beachwear spilled over from tables and jostled for position with household goods, rainbow coloured sweets and enormous panniers overflowing with fruit and vegetables. More practically I bought a vast quantity of fresh apricots at very low cost and later made enough jars of apricot chutney to last until the following year. I used a recipe from the Costa Blanca Times that was so delicious, even when I made it, that it became a family favourite. Chutney was one of the things we simply could not buy in Spain and as every lunch in summer consisted of a selection of cheeses and cold meats with fresh crusty bread, we just had to have a decent chutney; anyone who came to stay with us was asked to bring a few empty jars, preferably stuffed with Earl Grey tea. Of course the fruit was so expensive back in England that I could only justify making a few pounds of chutney when the apricots finally arrived in the British supermarkets.

However there was trouble in paradise and we gradually formed the impression that our house was being watched. Occasionally we began to feel that a malign scrutiny was upon us, particularly so one evening when we were enjoying an informal dinner party with friends on the pool terrace and we could sense eyes upon us from the hedges. Moreover Jeremy had noticed signs of tampering and petty pilfering around the property, even if we had been away from home for less than an hour. Jeremy was becoming increasingly angry and ever more determined to catch the culprit red handed, so every time we came home he would lock the children and me in the car, grab the heavy iron poker from beneath his seat and tear around the house brandishing it aloft.

Thank goodness he never did disturb anyone at the finca. Local newspapers were running stories of foreigners returning to their villas to discover intruders with sawn-off shotguns; further along the coast an Englishman had recently been killed by burglars. As you will soon read, the situation quickly became far more threatening.

With our young family in mind we eventually decided enough was enough: the time had come to move onto Seahawk for the remainder of our time in Spain. Letting go of La Abubilla would be a wrench, but the marina had 24-hour security, the boat was spacious and comfortable, moreover Moraira was a picturesque village with some good restaurants and its own bijou sandy beach at El Portet.

The move was made on the morning after a robbery that occurred just before the end of the summer term, when the finca was stripped almost bare. The end of term was still a few days away, but we desperately needed to escape and decided on the spur of the moment to take off for Ibiza for the week. Jeremy always kept the boat fully victualled and we only had to stock the fridges with a few fresh things, knowing we could eat out each evening. From the weekends we had spent on board Seahawk during the early summer, we already knew how surprisingly easy life afloat with our children could be; the children shared a cabin, where Jeremy had rigged up a cotton netting lee-cloth on Miranda's bunk to prevent her accidentally rolling onto Rory's double bed during the night. In the daytime Miranda's lobster pot playpen, filled with her favourite toys, was secured in Seakawk's large cockpit in the shade of the flying bridge, where she amused herself for hours, propped up in a corner of her playpen on a cushion of assorted blankets and teddy bears. Eight feet above her, Rory was always eager to keep watch from the helm position on the bridge.

As we set off under cornflower blue skies from Moraira the sea was calm enough, sparkling with a million flashing diamonds as it always does in the Mediterranean. Seahawk's chief advantage was speed, and with her powerful engines we arrived at the marina in Ibiza less than three hours later. After tea and late siesta we decided to take a leisurely amble into town, where we could choose a restaurant for supper as soon as the fierce heat had gone out of the sun. We had only walked a few hundred yards along the road around the head of the harbour when the most ghastly smell imaginable assailed us, a revolting mixture of sewage, rotting cabbages and dead animals. One glance at the filthy water confirmed our worst suspicions as we counted the bloated corpses of dogs, fish and even an unfortunate goat floating belly up on a blanket of raw sewage; there was hardly an inch of clear water to be seen.

The prevailing winds, Jeremy later explained, had blown this stinking tide of pollution into the farthest corner of the harbour, where it would remain until the weather changed; worse still, the same side of the harbour was in the midst of redevelopment, inconveniently turning the pavements into obstacle courses. We had all felt famished after so much sea air, but our appetites shrank away as we found ourselves gagging in the fearful miasma. We had already walked so far from the boat that we felt obliged to press on in the hope the smell would decrease nearer the town. I grabbed the packet of scented wet wipes from Miranda's changing bag and handed one each to Rory and Jeremy, keeping one for myself. We held them over our faces and charged as fast as we could towards the promise of fresh air. After a quick and unremarkable supper we repeated the Wet Wipe Run back to the boat and decided we would set off for the nearby deserted island of Espalmador at first light.

Jeremy had identified a promising anchorage that would be

sheltered from the swell and dropped Seahawk's anchor into ten feet of clear turquoise water. After a leisurely breakfast on board we took the dinghy ashore and unloaded the dazzling array of towels, baby paraphernalia, parasols, rugs, snacks, drinks, cold boxes, buckets and spades necessary for three short hours on a deserted beach – all these accoutrements absolutely vital, as Jeremy sarcastically pointed out, despite Seahawk's civilised amenities being thirty seconds away by dinghy. The soft, pale golden sand was tinged with pink at the water's edge and when I told Rory this colour was actually minute chippings of coral and shell, he insisted we bring a sieve from the galley on our next trip to the beach so he could begin a collection. After lunch and a short siesta on board we returned to the beach, where the quest for pink coral occupied Rory for the rest of the afternoon until he had filled an egg cup with tiny fragments.

On the way back to Ibiza each evening, I fed Miranda in the cockpit and gave her a wash in her pink plastic baby bath, which fitted neatly into the larger sink in the galley. Once back on our berth we showered and changed ready to visit the Old Town for supper. Remembering how attractive and fascinating the open air night street markets of Ibiza had been on our honeymoon in 1980, Jeremy and I were looking forward to seeing them again – one of us intent on buying some souvenirs. Thanks to the burglars we were all running very short of summer clothes, so I bought some beautiful outfits for the children, the Spanish fashions being so much more stylish and unusual than anything from England. I found a few casual summer outfits for myself, even one or two for Jeremy, and some very unusual handmade costume jewellery to replace some of my collection that had been stolen.

Fortunately the wind had changed direction by the time we walked from the boat on our second night and we reached the high walls of the Old Town without the need for wet wipes. Higher and higher we climbed through narrow winding streets, all awash with the accumulated heat of the day and the commotion of customers at the tables and chairs of bars and restaurants. Eventually we surfaced in the fresher solitude of the *mirador* behind the town hall, where we could take a moment's ease to admire the colossal views over the harbour and the distant islands to the south. Chance took us on a different route back into the melée until we found a small square fronted by a row of iron benches in the shade of a tangle of pine trees; beyond them a traditional old house with green shutters on its tall windows had been converted into an attractive restaurant, its tastefully laid tables set beneath pastel coloured parasols on the lane in front. *Las Ventanas* became our regular place to eat for the rest of our week in Ibiza; its choice had been set in stone when the Danish chef offered to cook *Crêpes Suzette* for Rory, despite the dish not appearing on their menu.

On the way through the Old Town Rory had noticed blackboards outside every other restaurant advertising Crêpes Suzette. Without the slightest clue what they were, he decided Crêpes Suzette was exactly what he wanted to eat. We tried in vain to persuade him to order his favourite onion rings, (our name for fried *calamare* where Rory was concerned, knowing the idea of squid would never tempt him when we first arrived in Spain), but he was adamant. Listening to our pleas, the waiter disappeared into the kitchen and came back with news that the chef would be delighted to cook Crêpes Suzette for Rory; better still, he could watch them being cooked and flamed if he so wished. Our delighted six year-old trotted off happily to the kitchen holding the waiter's hand and giving us a cheeky backward glance that said 'See!'. A short while later Rory reappeared with his waiter, followed by the statuesque Danish chef holding aloft a plate of sizzling crêpes. Rory finished every mouthful and promptly fell asleep on two cushioned chairs pushed together by the considerate waiter. For starters Jeremy and I enjoyed our first white gazpacho; served super-chilled in simple white china soup bowls, it was utterly delicious and perfectly refreshing in the heat. I can't recall our main course now, but I will never forget the first taste of homemade Crema Catalana – yet another of those sacrilegious novelties, like hummus, mozzarella, balsamic vinegar and Perrier, that were regarded as the Devil's work in the South Hams of the 1980's. On the long walk back to the marina Rory somehow squeezed most of himself into Miranda's pram, his legs dangling limp, and they both slept soundly until we carried them onto Seahawk and tucked them into their beds.

Chapter 7 – Jeremy
Mí Casa es Su Casa

A thief believes that everybody steals.

E.W. Howe

Much as Jani has already related, we had taken to our new home like field mice to a haystack; Rory was easily getting to grips with Spanish at his school in Jávea, while Miranda thrived on the novel experience of outdoor life without first being cocooned in layers of clothing like an onion. Early morning frosts and delicate mantles of mist would dissolve long before breakfast al fresco, the March sunshine already strong enough to send us scurrying for midday shade. The sublime peace of the deliciously scented valley was broken only by the twin carriage tram from Dénia to Alicante that very occasionally wheezed and groaned its lonely way sedately through the countryside whenever a blue moon coincided with a passing flight of pigs. Jani and I were quick to congratulate each other on our judicious and relatively straightforward move to Spain; indeed it was difficult to see what had prevented us from living abroad sooner. We were awash with smugness.

Our lives during the first months at La Abubilla were as perfect and uncomplicated as we could ever have hoped or imagined; since arriving in Spain, even in January, we were spending more time outdoors than we ever had during an entire English summer. Patches of early morning frost evaporated in the first rays of sun, leaving long days at our disposal without any thought of a raincoat, although Jani did have to buy a parasol for Miranda's pram. Our crystal clear pool remained far too cold for swimming until Jani and Rory insisted I bought an insulation cover; thereafter Jani was swimming every day as soon as the calendar turned to March. I was working my way down a long list of small improvements and repairs around the property, which usually entailed daily trips to the *ferreterias* in the area to look for particular bits and pieces. Spain was blessed with the best stocked stores I had ever seen – ironmongery porn of the highest grade, second only to chandlery smut as far as I was concerned. Invariably I wasted hours in these enticing tool brothels and came away with many items I would never need or use.

On the occasions when my journeys were not delayed by the attentions of the traffic police, other obstacles and delays often presented themselves. The strangest of these happened on one of the formal days of penance in Jesús Pobre. A solemn procession was in full swing behind a stern looking group of priests and local dignitaries as I drew up at the crossroads near the church. I had arrived a few moments too late to swerve in front of them and was left with no choice but to watch in ever increasing admiration and awe that gradually gave way to dismay and, finally, to anger. The votaries from the village (for I supposed it was they who had turned out in such numbers) were with few exceptions female, whereas the dignitaries and priests – surprise, surprise – were all men. As the penitents passed slowly a few feet in front of me, in order of misdemeanour I assumed, so the acts of contrition and mortification grew ever more extreme. Some way behind came the last old lady, seventy if a day, clawing her way with hands and elbows to drag her body along the road like a wounded animal whose legs had been shot away. What unspeakable sin she had committed to deserve this, I wondered? And how could any religion inflict such a humiliatingly public *auto-da-fé* upon its followers in this day and age? After the school run I was invariably sent on daily errands to find fresh milk – the one essential we could not forgo without entirely losing our composure. (There is very little so unsettling to the stomach as the sight, sound and smell of a globule of curdled milk plopping from milk carton onto a bowl of corn flakes first thing in the morning). It shouldn't have been a difficult task, given that every mini market stocked it – even on occasion the Hermit's Larder in Jesús Pobre – but the milk was invariably sour and often halfway to overripe camembert, despite the date stamp.

Occasionally I had to drive ten miles before I found a single carton that had been properly stored and was still sweet; I soon learned to taste the milk in front of the shopkeeper, often beating a hasty retreat after leaving a trail of opened cartons and angry staff behind me as I left each shop. It reminded me of the violent illness that had struck many yachtsmen in Barbados a decade earlier – the island being one of the preferred landfalls for yachts crossing the Atlantic. After weeks at sea the crews were desperate for any food that hadn't come out of a tin, so the unremarkable supermarket closest to the dinghy landing in Bridgetown became the yachties' shopping destination of choice. After an official investigation into the cause of so many debilitating stomach bugs, the illness was traced to this particular shop, where it was discovered the overzealous Bajan manager had decided to save electricity by switching off all the fridges and freezer cabinets before he locked up each night.

In Spain the leading dairy companies distributed fresh

pasteurused milk in cartons throughout the land and, assuming they didn't instruct their lorry drivers to turn off the refrigeration en route, it was difficult to discern where the fault lay. And yet in Cyprus, so much hotter than Spain, we had never encountered any rancid milk problems; better still we could also buy proper Greek yogurt from the market every single day of the year. This unpasteurised yogurt, at once deliciously tangy and creamy, came in crude earthenware pint-sized pots, glazed on the inside, which were duly returned to the market for re-use. A plain circle of greaseproof paper attached with string was all that covered the firm crust, despite which I can only remember one occasion in two years when the contents had to be thrown away. Jani and I took our lead from our Cypriot friends, who consumed prodigious quantities of yogurt with each and every savoury meal, as well as with nuts, fresh fruit and honey; sadly health and safety directives have long since put paid to all such fortifying doses of bacteria that once bolstered our immune systems.

Tim and Din, our old friends from Devon came to stay with us in May. The nights had become increasingly mild since Christmas and, as we returned from a restaurant in Dénia on their first evening at La Abubilla, I casually asked Jani if she had meant to leave the doors open on the pretty Hansel and Gretel balcony outside our bedroom.

"Actually *you* were the last one out of the house a*nd* you managed to leave the light on. Now the place will be crawling with bugs … How could you!", she replied as the party unfolded themselves from the back of our overcrowded car. Unlocking the iron gate and heavy front door I stepped inside the house and immediately tripped over an upturned drawer.

"I'm afraid it's more than insect life that's been in here," I answered, picking up a heavy poker from the fireplace and creeping gingerly upstairs between the debris scattered by the intruders. "Was it Red Indians, Rory?" asked our guests' young son in wide eyed horror, imagining a raiding party of tomahawk wielding Native Americans from a Sunday afternoon movie, inevitably starring John Wayne.

"I suppose this is what Roy's brother must have meant by *occasional trouble with vagrants*," I ventured sardonically, looking around at our ransacked belongings and capsized furniture.

The rear courtyard doors had been smashed open, their protective iron bars bent apart like plasticine; upstairs the wardrobes had been emptied onto the floor and the mattresses flung from our beds; thankfully our friends soon returned from the casita to report it untouched and intact. Urging them to lock their shutters and leave all outside lights switched on throughout the night, they seemed remarkably unperturbed.

"I can't cope with all this now," sobbed Jani, "but we're not sleeping in sheets those revolting people have touched. Everything will have to be washed, even the toys. I feel so horribly dirty… You don't think they'll come back, do you?"

"Not a chance, darling. They've got what they came for and in any case these scum are invariably cowards." I answered confidently. We found some spare linen and put the children to bed between us, Jani eventually succumbing to exhaustion while I dozed nervously with the poker still tightly gripped in my trembling hand.

On closer inspection the thieves had taken very little of consequence; I surmised the approaching loom of our headlights swinging down the valley must have disturbed them before they could get properly stuck in. A few hundred in sterling had been taken from my desk and some electrical goods had also vanished, but it was the theft of our privacy and security that left us with such a strong feeling of violation and defilement. Our French windows were duly reglazed and their heavy iron grills reinforced over the following days, while Jani washed and sanitised the entire house with fifty-seven varieties of disinfectant. Gradually life returned onto an even keel and as the weeks passed we began to enjoy our scented valley once more. In fact we decided the burglary was a cause for celebration, for we had already suffered our fire and now we could also confidently tick burglary off the list of expected mishaps. After all, lightning would never strike twice.

A few weeks later we were joined by our old friends Vanessa and Stefan with their daughter Sara, who had been born on the very same day as Miranda. They had flown in from Munich, where Stefan ran a very successful advertising business; Jani had unwittingly introduced the happy couple to each other on a beach in Ibiza. Several years ago Vanessa had asked Jani to recommend somewhere suitable for a short holiday, following a bust up with a boyfriend; unhesitatingly Jani suggested Cala Vedella, the beach she and I remembered so fondly from our honeymoon on Aries eight years earlier. Sure enough Vanessa had flown to Ibiza and taken a room above the beach, where chance found her on a sunbed next to Stefan the very next day. Hesitant conversation in a foreign language had begun awkwardly for them both, but romance, engagement, marriage and a daughter soon followed in quick succession.

We collected the three of them from Alicante airport in the

morning and had been enjoying our first leisurely lunch together in the shade of the *naya* beside the pool, when Stefan strolled back to the casita for his camera. Moments later he returned ashen faced with the news that his camera, wallet, tickets, cash, Vanessa's handbag and some jewellery were all missing. My heart sank as I understood immediately that burglars had struck again. But how? We had been sitting just forty paces from the carefully locked casita.

On the casita's sitting room floor we found a trail of broken glass leading to the bathroom, where we discovered the ventilation window and the steel bars protecting it had been pulled clean out of the wall. I fought my way past the cactus and prickly pears at the back of the casita and found the sturdy ironwork and window frame lying in the undergrowth. Further inspection revealed tyre tracks in the baked earth of our uncultivated field beyond – silent witnesses to the method used to haul the window from the masonry of the ancient wall with a long rope. Somehow the culprits had accomplished all this without alerting us to a single squeak. But as Stefan and I sagely concluded later that evening, as we drowned our sorrows in several carafes of wine, our wives had not paused to draw breath since their effusive reunion at the airport that morning. Amid such incessant and animated chatter Hannibal's entire army, complete with elephants, could have trampled through our silent valley undetected.

Jani and I were mortified by our friends' misfortune, for which we naturally felt entirely responsible. Luckily for them, and with impeccable German efficiency, their losses were all fully insured; but unluckily for us it was impossible to obtain any insurance to cover Spanish thievery and vandalism, no matter how many hideous steel bars and shutters we might be persuaded to fit. We didn't know it at the time, but the greatest single expense during our time in Spain, other than the value of property stolen, would be the costs of repairing damage to our doors, walls and windows. More generally the reasons for the presence of steel bars on every single window in Spain had never crossed my mind; to me the iron grills were simply a part of the landscape, even if I had never seen these hideous fortifications in noteworthy profusion in other European countries. Obviously, I concluded, the Spaniards found them attractive features, like window boxes; or perhaps they were maintained as salutary reminders of the Civil War and subsequent dictatorships that had kept the entire Iberian peninsula in its iron grip until so recently. Why hadn't I considered the obvious threats suggested by these unsightly defenses before we bought such an isolated property?

Both our burglaries had coincided with the arrival of friends coming to stay with us; obviously our movements and activities had been noticed and we were becoming increasingly suspicious about the more stand-offish of our Spanish neighbours dotted around the valley. Perhaps, where newcomers were concerned, they had unilaterally decided to replace their delightfully hospitable Spanish maxim, *Mi casa es su casa, (my house is your house)* with a more threatening *Su cash es mi cash.*

Shortly after we had moved to La Abubilla Jani had taken on a 'Mrs Flapduster' from the village. Maria had arrived out of the blue one morning to ask if she might return to work at our finca, where she had been employed as a cleaner by the previous owners; at the time we could see no reason to send her away and she began her duties immediately. Tut-tutting at the state of the old clay tiles on the ground floor, Maria patiently explained – as near as we could understand from her colloquial accent – that we needed Bald O'Pinky to come and clean them thoroughly and bring out their attractive colour and patina. We had no idea who she was talking about, but admitted we had struggled with the floor; water seemed to degrade the surface of the tiles and nothing we had tried made them look any less dowdy. So we asked Maria to bring Señor O'Pinky along with her the following day, fully expecting her to be accompanied by a shaven-headed, painfully sunburnt Irishman with a derogatory nickname. But no, all was revealed when she appeared the next morning with a large drum of golden sealant labelled *Baldopinky – Mejor para baldosas*, (best for tiles), which she expertly sloshed over the floors to astonishing effect. Thereafter Maria came to do the housework twice a week, always smartly if inappropriately dressed for church, in faded black widows' weeds, with her hair in a prim bun, wearing a permanent expression of silent disapproval as she fruitlessly flapped the dust from one surface to the next. Naturally enough, and here was the point, she was also asked to make up the beds in the casita whenever guests were expected.

A month or so before our first burglary, during those carefree days when we could do no wrong, Jani had called in for coffee at Roy and Gill's villa one morning. At some point the name of our new maid was mentioned in conversation, whereupon Jani immediately noticed a cloud passing over her friend's brow. Nothing more was ever said until the day after we had suffered the indignity of our second burglary, when Roy had telephoned me to pass on his concerns in confidence. Maria, he suggested, was the only person who would have been aware of our guests' impending arrivals. Whether as an ill-disposed informant or merely as a gossip who spent too much time chatting in the village, she was the likeliest link to our two robberies. If there had been more tangible evidence to impute Maria's trustworthiness it was never mentioned; and although this was hardly a firm denunciation it was decided to dispense with her flapdusting services forthwith. Putting suspicion and the possibility of her innocence to one side, we would not miss Maria's imperious demands for another hour's pay if ever her time was exceeded by a minute or two, but more importantly Rory had loathed her on sight. (Never ignore your young children when they inexplicably take an instant dislike to an adult!)

Tranquility quickly returned to our valley, but neither of us would admit how unsettled we had become after the second burglary. Our general unease was further increased by a noticeable aloofness and lack of empathy from the locals and shopkeepers in the village. Politeness was always there, but it was cursory and suffused with an unmistakeable undercurrent of wariness; had we been in Southern Italy it would have been called *omertà*. Miguel the gardener had engaged with us in his simple way from the beginning, but he too was a stranger to the area who confessed to finding the locals *muy aislados*, very insular. The only other Spaniard who gave us the time of day was the branch manager of our bank in the village – I can't imagine why. To be fair the local Catalan dialect in the valley could be difficult to follow and bore little resemblance to the precise Castilian Spanish we strove to learn, so our inability to converse beyond the daily exchange of greetings put us at an obvious disadvantage while our ears attuned. Moreover the entire population of the village seemed remarkably decrepit to us youngsters and appeared to come from a different and evidently more parochial era in which youthful foreigners might not be so welcome. Perhaps they still bore a grudge against the English for betraying the Catalans at the Treaty of Utrecht or, within living memory, for refusing to arm their elected government during the Civil War.

Certainly the curiosity and effusive congeniality of the many Greeks we had come to know so well in Cyprus (a joy that would be multiplied tenfold in Corfu a decade later) was disappointingly missing, as was their generosity of spirit and demonstrative affection. Above all we missed the blithe state of chaos and benign anarchy that permeated every aspect of Greek life; in our corner of Spain these delights had been replaced by a stern, authoritarian correctness that seemed entirely out of place in any Mediterranean country. Was it us, or had we walked into some longstanding local feud concerning La Abubilla? We never would find out for certain and if the locals knew they weren't telling. Actually, come to think of it, I couldn't recall noticing Maria's puritanical face amongst the crowd of penitents at that solemn procession in Jesús Pobre. Despite its fierce sunshine we were beginning to understand that Spain could often be a cold country.

At the end of May, just as we had begun to relax, our finca was targeted again. After a dinner party with friends we returned to find the kitchen door off its hinges and the steel bars of the outer door neatly cut asunder. Once again the burglars must have been disturbed by our return and only a silver candelabra was missing from the dining table. Thoroughly fed up and resigned to the situation I propped some furniture against the broken door and went upstairs to find both children in bed with Jani; I tried to get some sleep in Rory's bed, but but I was far too angry to settle and spent most of the night planning ever stronger fortifications. Surely something more could be done to protect our home. Ian, our friend latterly from Northampton, had once asked for some electric fencing to deter animals from entering his back garden, whereupon the perceptive shopkeeper had asked whether the animals were of the two-legged variety. Would it be illegal, I pondered, to electrify the iron grills fitted to every door and window of our finca? And would 50,000 volts be considered unreasonable? Ian had also suggested we left some cash on the hall table in the hope the burglars would settle for that and look no further; then again one of our fellow parents from school favoured fitting an alarm, unaware that nobody in our valley would ever take heed of any bell smaller than Big Ben.

I decided it was time to speak to the local Guardia Civil in Gata de Gorgos and drove there before lunch the next day. The officer in charge turned out to be dapper and taciturn, with a deadpan expression that failed to conceal the weary resignation of a man ready for retirement. I complimented him on his excellent English and learnt that he had been sent away to London for several years during his childhood to escape the Civil War – his father being uncertain as to which side was going to emerge victorious. As we sat down I asked him what might be done to prevent the further attentions of our determined vagrants.

"*Señor.* Not one month ago I myself was robbed as I slept in my own bed," he began patiently. "Most of my wife's jewellery was taken and, if you understand that I cannot even promise her it will never happen again, then you will see there is very little I can do for you. You can guard your house like the Alcázar and these *ladrones* will always find a way to rob you. Now is the robbing season."

Pausing to light the stub of a dry cheroot the officer grimaced as his lazy gaze rose to a faded portrait of Generalissimo Franco on the flaking wall beside us, within which I detected his yearning for a long lamented era of authoritarian orderliness.

"Our government has often tried to break up these gangs, but around here it would be easier to find an honest lawyer," he continued sympathetically. "These wanderers are professionals. They descend like locusts from the slums of our cities, the *malos barrios*, to our coasts; they select a target – a *gordo*, a fat one, or sometimes a lonely little house like yours – they watch and wait a little, they strike and then they melt away like a frost in April. They're probably camped out in the countryside nearby and what's more you will probably have passed them in your village street without knowing it."

Glancing at his watch he stood up to show me out. It was time for his siesta.

"Also you should understand," he suddenly added, gripping my shoulder as we walked to the door, "these are very dangerous people! You must never attempt to confront them when they return."

"Return?" I asked in astonishment. "You mean they'll strike again?"

"But of course! This is only a question of time. Why do you think nobody can get insurance for remote houses like yours? I hope and pray you never disturb them," he replied warily.

"So you're telling me there's nothing to be done?"

"Well, perhaps I might suggest you leave your doors unlocked. After all, you say there is nothing left of any great value in the house ..." he paused briefly with an actorly shrug of the shoulders, spreading his palms upwards in acquiescence before resuming more brightly, "… then at least you would save yourself the cost of repairs."

For a fraction of a second I thought he was pulling my leg. Perhaps I might also pin a message to the front door inviting any passing criminals to help themselves to the key under the flower pot, should the urge to steal something become irresistible – there's cold beer in the fridge.

This was news I dared not share with Jani until much later on, (as with the six-foot long Montpelier snake I had once seen slithering its way up the wall and disappearing like a tube train into a convenient gap beneath the roof tiles above our bedroom). Nevertheless she and Rory must have wondered why I would always lock them in the car whenever we returned home while I hurriedly searched the house, brandishing the heavy poker I kept beside the driver's seat. I never did disturb any burglar, which was probably just as well because one of us would surely have killed the other. Usually I would find the finca intact, but on two further occasions our dear little casita suffered the same familiar treatment, leaving a door or shutter reduced to matchsticks and a trail of havoc within.

When our nerves became too frayed after one of these incidents we would spend a few days on the boat to regain our composure. Reassuringly we began to feel safe as soon as the guard at the marina entrance closed the barrier behind our car, although this was hardly the Spanish way of life Jani and I could ever have envisaged. Nevertheless returning to the finca after a sojourn afloat was always a pleasure; La Abubilla was an utterly charming place to live and our confidence inexplicably soared as soon as we unlocked each door and threw open the shutters. Surely the latest hardened steel locks and stainless steel chains would defeat our would-be intruders from now on. Surely, we earnestly hoped, our luck would change and we would be left alone in peace.

June was flying by and suddenly the summer holidays were about to burst upon us. More friends had come to stay at La Abubilla without any further incident and an avalanche of visitors were threatening to descend in July ... perhaps our prized telephone line hadn't been such a blessing after all. Calls to England were fearfully expensive, but they must have been far more reasonable in the opposite direction, judging by the number of friends who telephoned to ask when our casita might be free. I had tried to save some money by experimenting with the old trick of tapping the telephone cradle to dial foreign numbers – one tap for the numeral 1, two taps for 2 and so on – but the calls were charged to our bill nevertheless and I had to assume the trick only worked on old fashioned analogue receivers. The system had worked perfectly from the nearest inconspicuous telephone box to my public school, (a four mile bike ride into the wilderness, phone calls being strictly forbidden), and it also worked years later from one particular payphone in the south of Gran Canaria, where a queue of yachties soon lined up to call home before setting off across the Atlantic. I should have charged a fee for my expert tapping tutorials.

(The mass arrival of mobile phones in the 1990's came as a great blessing – generally speaking. Miranda was given her first Nokia when she started at Millfield; it would, after all, keep her in touch with us at all times. She called us every evening during her first week, but the communications soon slowed to a dribble and we assumed all was well. Then we got the first bill for her number: over two hundred pounds for one month! This was a colossal sum of money at the time. After some serious questioning we discovered Miranda was not only calling her friends in other boarding houses, she was constantly texting girls in the bedrooms next door, and even the girl with whom she shared her luxurious room.)

We intended to return to England in August when the children would find the soaring temperatures far less tolerable; but in the meantime the first of several trips to Ibiza, and later to Menorca, were eagerly anticipated. End of term fixtures at Rory's school included an ambitious production of The Wizard of Oz at a theatre in Jávea. Many of the mothers including Jani had been involved with last minute backstage preparations on the day, so we had all been away from La Abubilla for many hours by the time we got home in the evening to find our heavy front door had been jemmied wide open; its solid oak timbers had survived the onslaught unscathed, but an inferior, more modern frame had been no match for our determined intruders.

Stepping over splinters of wood in the hall I switched on the lights. Within the main room I encountered a scene resembling wreckage from a shipwreck, strewn like matchwood on a beach. The floors were scattered with capsized furniture and upturned drawers, their contents rifled and thrown about the rooms in a show of gratuitous contempt; upstairs the mattresses had been upended from the beds, our wardrobes ransacked and the mosquito screens slashed. A few remaining books and many of my clothes had been tossed about the floor – evidently they hadn't found favour. From a single glance around all this carnage it was obvious that most our belongings had been taken: the children's clothing and toys, a trove of cosmetics, most of Jani's clothes and costume jewellery, some silver and even a couple of smaller pieces of furniture had all gone. Fortunately Jani and I had long since learnt to take our passports and bank cards with us wherever we went.

Most alarmingly Rory had been the first to discover a large carving knife discarded on his mattress, the sight of which must have conjured up menacing visions of pirates determinedly scaling the walls to his bedroom, with cutlasses between their teeth. I cleared up the mess while Jani did her best to settle the children, who fortunately were both dead on their feet after such a busy day. In fact there was little I could do except push the damaged furniture into one corner, salvage some paperwork and sweep up the mess of broken ornaments, picture frames, table lamps and goodness knows what else that had been thrown to the floor. As Jani came down the stairs we both halted in our tracks and looked at each other, already knowing that our unspoken anxieties had led us both to the same inevitable conclusion.

"Why don't we move onto Seahawk until things settle down," I calmly suggested, not wishing to draw a final line under our Spanish sabbatical too hastily. "After all we were planning to go over to Ibiza next weekend anyway. We could move out of here properly when we get back; at least we know the marina's completely safe."

"I was thinking more of moving aboard tonight, actually," replied Jani testily.

"Yes, but that's not realistic at this time of night, is it," I reasoned. "So let's leave for the boat early tomorrow morning and scoot straight over to Ibiza. Seahawk's always ready to go and we could be there by teatime! Rory will miss the last couple of days of term, but who cares at his age. Then we can bring forward our trip home to Devon as soon as we get back."

Seeing I was making little headway I quickly added the S word.

"You could also shop for some new clothes in Ibiza; you love the street markets and shops over there, especially the children's boutiques … and there's so much stolen clothing to replace now." Jani's brow cleared slightly as we continued the horrid business of tidying up.

"Alright, but after tonight that's it. I'm not spending another night in this godforsaken place, shopping or no shopping," muttered Jani as she disappeared up the stone stairs with an armful of clean sheets from the bathroom cupboard that had somehow escaped the burglars' attentions. "There must be some jinx or vendetta … A house near Jesús Pobre, indeed! … No wonder Jesús was poor … He obviously got robbed silly when he was here too … Trust us to find it!"

The game, I knew, was well and truly up. Early the following morning I called the removal firm who had efficiently brought our furniture from Devon barely five months earlier. I explained the situation and authorised them to pack up and collect whatever remained of our belongings during our week's absence in Ibiza. As we left for the marina I glanced back at the pretty, innocent little house, wondering if the extra chains and padlocks hastily bought from the *ferretería* that morning would protect it until our return. For the hell of it I composed a curt message in my best schoolboy Spanish, adding a translation as an afterthought as I stapled it to the front gate.

¡TODO YA ROBADO – NO HAY NADA AQUÍ!
EVERYTHING ALREADY STOLEN –
THERE'S NOTHING LEFT HERE!

Clearing the marina entrance at lunchtime I opened Seahawk's throttles and set the autopilot on its course for the narrow channel between Espalmador and Ibiza, some 75 miles distant. The lofty haunches of Montgó and Cabo de la Nao quickly receded into the shimmering summer haze as our worries dissolved temporarily into the sparkling white ribbon of the boat's long, foaming wake. Two hours later six year-old Rory, standing able watch on the bridge, spotted the 400-metre pinnacle of Isla Vedra emerging out of the heat haze like a finger beckoning us onwards. Before another hour had passed Seahawk was comfortably moored at the north-eastern side of Ibiza harbour in good time for afternoon tea under the welcome shade of the cockpit awnings.

* * *

I had first visited Ibiza with my parents in 1962 when, on a whim, my mother Liz had decided to buy an astonishingly cheap Ibizincan farmhouse. With the ruins of an even older watch tower rising over one end of its crumbling structure, the property had gloriously uninterrupted views over the string of islands between Formentera and Ibiza Town. This was to be an investment project to replace her beloved Kensington home, which she had most reluctantly sold to help Michael improve the farm ten years earlier. Liz had inherited an architect's eye from her father, a shrewd nose for a good investment from her grandfather, a director of The Prudential, and a buccaneering spirit from … actually we never did discover where that came from.

During the late 1950's she and Michael had travelled in smoldering silence on similar sorties to look for property in

Perigueux, Cavalaire and Saint-Paul-de-Vence; but this, as a thirteen year-old adolescent with growing pains and a low boredom threshold, was my first trip abroad with my parents. Michael – always tipped into cantankerous mood at the first hint of continental, garlic-ridden fare – was determined to come along for the ride, if only to pour scorn upon my mother's latest scheme at every opportunity. His unrelenting pessimism could always be relied upon to supply countless reasons to plunge the rosiest of prospects for any of his family's proposed endeavours into an ocean of red ink; if his initial cautions and forebodings fell on deaf ears his mood would boil over into hopping, bug-eyed fury until the rest of us either acquiesced or continued without his knowledge. Liz had contrived to leave him behind on this occasion, but the old dog in the manger had even deserted his favourite brood mare to keep a beady eye on us both.

So despite the strong probability of another wild goose chase, the three of us and our luggage squeezed into Liz's raucous Morris Mini Cooper to drive south from Devon to Barcelona through the blazing August heat. Michael had insisted the Mini was more suitable for the dirt roads of Ibiza than his lumbering Mark IX Jaguar; but in fact the truth owed more to the novel rarity and raffishness of the brand new Mini, and further to my father's unilaterally observed convention that the owner of a car always paid for its petrol. Oddly enough I had been more than content to wedge myself between the suitcases in the back of the tiny Mini, since the commodious back seat of the Jaguar smelt like an odious commode – having frequently been occupied by petrified and incontinent Jersey bull calves on their final journey from farm to slaughterhouse. Michael had never in his entire life caused any of his motor cars to be cleaned either inside or out, preferring instead to replace them only when levels of congealed mud, straw and ordure in the footwell rendered safe operation of the pedals impossible. (His reasoning changed in later life, when a respectable dent on all four corners of the car was all the encouragement he needed to buy a new model. As he approached his mid-nineties each gleaming replacement would rarely survive its first month on the road before the bumpers looked as if they had come off second best in a fight with a bulldozer.)

Once behind the wheel, as I may have mentioned earlier, Michael could rarely be diverted from the road ahead; the frugal mini-car bestowed lamentably few refueling stops upon us as we scorched noisily southwards along the poplar lined *routes nationales* of France, shading our eyes against the painful, stroboscopic pulses of sunshine flickering and flashing between the tall trees. He had always claimed to know France like the back of his hand; but instead, aided by a faithful copy of *Michelin* dating from the 1930's that had accompanied him through the final months of the war, he succeeded in adding three blazing arguments, one hideous night amidst the bedbugs in an expensive hotel that should have known better, and several hundred kilometres to our journey. Half starved, deafened, dazed and irritable, my parents appeared more estranged than a pair of alabaster bookends as we turned at last through the gates of the grubby Barcelona docks. There, under the floodlights our car was clumsily enfolded in a cargo net like a matchbox toy and precariously hoisted aboard a rustbucket ferry bound for Ibiza.

Our ears were still ringing when we awoke next morning to find the ferry safely alongside the old dock in Ibiza port, where a dingy bar on the quayside next to the customs shed catered mainly for the stevedores as they idly awaited their next ship.

We sat outside this shack in an involuntary silence brought on by the torrid August heat, marveling at the enchanting view of the old town rising above us like a clumsily decorated wedding cake, while we waited impatiently for the Mini to be lifted from the hold. Our rickety table and chairs sat on ill-fitting boards straddling the gully of an open sewer that lazily disgorged itself into the harbour beside us, where shoals of mullet lazily grazed on the effluent; as I sat there contentedly swinging my legs, sipping glass after glass of iced grenadine through a freshly cut reed straw that transformed the syrupy cordial into exquisite nectar, I quickly became engrossed in my own graphically realistic game of Pooh Sticks. Perhaps, I pondered as only an adolescent could, there might be something for me to enjoy in Ibiza after all.

My instinct proved correct, manifested in the shape of two Vespa motor scooters; they had been thoughtfully provided at our faraway, rustic quarters for the purpose of exploring the island's turquoise embroidered coasts otherwise inaccessible by car. In those days many of the island's remoter communities and untouched beaches were approachable only by goat tracks that twisted down through pine-scented hillsides to a sea still undefiled by the looming tide of plastic litter. I had been riding our stockman's elderly BSA around the farm since I was eleven, and Michael assured us that his experience on army motorbikes would quickly return; however Liz wasn't so sure and her concerns about our first serious foray into the hills proved more than justified. As our first ascent through a pine forest grew ever steeper, Michael's battle with the Vespa's hand-operated gear change and clutch was quickly lost; eventually he came to a stuttering halt on the steepest and narrowest part of the track, where it was impossible to turn around. Determined not to be outdone, Michael finally found first gear, revved up the clattering engine and popped the clutch.

Instantly the scooter reared up like a whipped stallion, unceremoniously unshipping my hapless father before careering away deep into the thickets beside us. Liz, who had already transferred to my pillion for her own safety, could no longer contain herself any more than I as Michael completed several backwards tumbles down the hillside, before nimbly regaining his feet with the startled expression of a cat that has just had a cold thermometer inserted up its bottom. The struggle to keep my scooter upright was instantly lost as my mother and I toppled over into paroxysms of helpless laughter. Thereafter Michael developed a sudden interest in the mould-speckled selection of novels displayed in our finca, while my mother and I enjoyed the delights of two-wheeled freedom together on the unmapped network of tracks that ran through the sparsely populated west side of the island. Poor Michael never did see the funny side of his antics with the scooter; nor did my mother ever let him forget them.

Spain had only flirted with the creeping European liberalisation of the early 1960's, but the handily detached island of Ibiza had long since raised two fingers to Franco's authoritarian regime and had been welcoming a motley band of bohemian artists and writers to its shores since the 1950's. One such, a costumier friend from the Rambert days, had alerted Liz to the bargain farmhouse and it was she who had loaned us her own charmingly primitive finca. Unlike its neighbour Formentera, Ibiza had not yet developed into the notorious haven for hippies and hippie watchers. Certainly the parched countryside surrounding us, an uncultivated wilderness in the back of beyond, was devoid of any sign of humanity apart from ourselves – although we did once catch sight of a ragged countryman falling out of an olive tree, so shocked was he to see the Mini racing past in a cloud of dust as he reached into the higher branches. Half empty shelves in the dusty backstreet shops of the island's capital displayed only a grim offering of fly-blown chicken carcasses and salt cod, tinned milk, weevil infested rice and a suspicious, yellow train oil masquerading as butter. Tomato omelettes supplemented by strictly rationed portions of Heinz baked beans, (stealthily secreted beneath the spare wheel in the Mini's boot), became my staple for breakfast and lunch. Fortunately Liz always insisted we drove the Mini into Ibiza Town or San Antonio Abad to find somewhere for supper.

True to form Michael loathed every minute of our refreshingly spartan holiday and did his utmost to spoil the fortnight for everyone else; he, after all, had grown up with far more exclusive vacations, the ski parties in Lech, the grand ocean liners and the private charters down the Eastern Adriatic with wildfowl and boar in the crosshairs. In comparison my mother's childhood holidays had never been quite as lavish as those of her malcontent husband, but her sunny disposition always allowed her to make the very best of whatever life threw at her.

As my mother often reminded me, some allowance had to be made for Michael's remote and dispiriting manner, even if it was painfully obvious that he didn't much care for either of us; for despite the trappings of immense privilege he had endured a cruelly challenging childhood aggravated by an enlarged heart that left him bedridden for several years. Deprived of those formative early teenage terms at Harrow, and bitter ever after, he was unwilling to show any signs of affection, enjoyment or fulfilment to his family. The pity of it was that he wished the same debilitating flaws upon us. That fondly remembered holiday in 1963 marked, I believe, the moment I encouraged a portion of rashness to enter my life – so determined was I to shake off the influence of a father who was content to fritter away the greater part of his life. Michael had no friends, but any of his acquaintances would have found these revelations hard to believe, for Michael generally presented a genial hail-fellow-well-met persona whenever he was able to socialise without the embarrassing presence of his family.

Much to my dismay Liz never did buy the simple farmhouse with its tower on a hilltop above Cala Talamanca; she and I had fallen for it completely, but Michael had thrown too many obstacles in the way, as always determined to keep my mother within sight and under control at all times. It went for a song and eventually became the lavish holiday retreat of some graceless rock star. In retrospect the Ibiza I had come to know in 1962 was that rare, unvarnished destination any one of us would now willingly kill for. Eighteen years later in 1980, when Jani and I sailed into Ibiza during our honeymoon passage to Cyprus on Aries, my recollections of the unspoilt, somewhat impoverished island bore little resemblance to the fast developing port and sprawling resorts.

* * *

Now in 1988, revisiting the island fleshpot with our own children after a further eight year interlude, our gin gazebo was finally in its element amidst its chrome and tinted glass siblings. Each morning at first light we would slip our exorbitantly expensive mooring and take off to the dazzling shell-pink beaches of Espalmador and Formentera; there Rory could gain confidence in the calm clear water while Miranda, still only nine months old, splashed contentedly beneath her halo of platinum blonde curls in the bath-warm shallows. Our days fell into a loose pattern, spending mornings on the beach until the sun became too fierce, then returning for lunch and a siesta on Seahawk until another session of paddling and swimming became irresistible. We soon learned the tiny island of Espalmador boasted a renowned mud bath at its centre, to which curious yachties and ageing hippies alike made their regular pilgrimage throughout each day. This dried up lagoon allegedly held healing and aphrodisiac properties that evidently outweighed the sulphurous stench that accompanied each of the slime blackened mud bathers as they returned past us on the beach.

One afternoon an extremely elderly and astonishingly tall skeleton of a man, stark naked, wrinkled as a discarded walnut shell and supported at either side by two well-endowed blonde dolly birds in a similar state of undress, made his faltering way along the beach towards the quagmire; some time later the trio reappeared out of the parched scrub behind us and staggered painfully slowly over the hot sand towards the sea to wash. Long before they reached the water's edge the hot sun had baked the black ooze into a hard, grey carapace and the old boy only just made it before he was transformed, like Lot's wife, into a freshly baked cadaver-en-croute. This gruesome spectacle, the cause of much animated pointing and exclamation from young Rory, brought to mind a whole new definition of the word *codpiece*. I still wonder to this day if he and his nubile assistants ever felt the benefit.

Each evening Jani's promised shopping therapy involved a long and unwholesome walk into town from the marina around the perimeter of the harbour, where the miasma of raw sewage was all too familiar from my first encounter almost thirty years earlier. Indeed the only way to negotiate these overpoweringly noxious vapours was to sprint with Miranda's pram before us like unwilling competitors in some hideously sadistic parents' race – so often the highlight of a school sports day – towards the promise of sweeter air. Once through these fetid furlongs we claimed our reward as we reached the cobbled streets of the old town. There the market stalls of the former hippie markets had reinvented themselves more commercially and slightly less exotically over the years, but as we climbed the donkey steps that wound their way up through the old town we rediscovered the original charm of the place shining through in spades.

Six days later we pointed Seahawk's bow towards our home port on the mainland, diverting briefly from our course for a sentimental swim at Cala Vedella. My first visit to this deep inlet in 1962 had been made by scooter along a track through the pine trees, when my mother and I had the golden sands to ourselves as we ate a simple picnic of bread, cheese and cool grenadine. I couldn't remember any buildings other than the fishermen's shacks at the top of the beach, only pine forests and cicadas. But as Seahawk dropped anchor amongst the clutter of small yachts in the bay, Jani and I stood aghast before the amphitheatre of concrete development above the beach, where a string of noisy bars buzzed with customers. (Let's face it, a beach can be sheer hell without loud music.)

Beside us on the water a group windsurfing lesson was concluding with a final exhortation to 'bend-ze-knees', or whatever the appropriate command might be in German. It was hardly restful, but we were fortunate to be afloat, where we could swim from the bathing platform on Seahawk's stern; once in the water, where the view of the freshly concreted hillsides were shielded by our boat's hull, we could pretend nothing had changed in the name of progress. As Jani and I had often concluded, the coastlines of most countries are most favourably viewed from the sea. From five miles out, on a fine day and given a favourable light, Torbay can resemble the Côte d'Azur; even Hull can appear quaintly welcoming and mysterious from the deck of a yacht running for shelter from a North Sea gale, in the depths of a black winter's night.

Our short cruise had reinvigorated us enormously; by the time Seahawk tied up again at its home berth at Moraira we had all but forgotten the evil spell that had settled so arbitrarily upon us a week earlier. That evening we returned to inspect La Abubilla and found everything surprisingly intact and orderly; the English removal firm had efficiently emptied the house in our absence, leaving only a jumbled pile of my old clothes the burglars had most insultingly rejected. Our 'vagrants' had obviously moved on to fresh hunting grounds and the finca seemed suddenly forlorn and unloved. Denied its daily tipple of chlorine our swimming pool had reverted from polished cerulean to a gloomy Atlantic green; beside it the lower courtyard was once again a swirling confetti of unswept leaves from the rampant purple and scarlet bougainvillea.

An air of perfect tranquility seemed to have settled over our valley, much as we had first found the property just a few months earlier. Perhaps we had been too hasty after all, but our furniture was already on its journey north to England, where we too were bound the following evening. The six hundred mile journey to the ferry terminal at Santander would be made on country roads through the centre of Spain, rather than along the partially completed motorway by way of Barcelona, where it petered out and turned into a roadworks jamboree thereafter. With a car heavily laden with luggage I was not looking forward to the tortuous journey through the night.

True to form Jani had shopped most enthusiastically on her family's behalf in Ibiza. The hippie markets had replaced their beads-and-joss-sticks theme with a more conventional fare that was still pleasingly quirky; and the wearable fashions from the more reasonable boutiques always came in the subtle colours from the Mediterranean palette to set them apart. Even I could see their appeal – they were so cheerfully un-English. With limited space to finish tidying up the boat I had decided to leave the four holdalls of goodies from Ibiza at the finca overnight; they were stuffed with all our new clothes and shoes, a handbag or two and several rolls of undeveloped film from our holiday. Another bag already packed from Seahawk contained all the oilskins, puddle jumpers and thick sweaters suitable for our forthcoming exposure to an English summer. Back at La Abubilla I crammed all five pieces of luggage into the airing cupboard, from where I would pick them up late the following evening before our tedious drive through the night. Both children would be fast asleep on the back seats by then, stretched out on top of lumpy mattresses of essential luggage from the boat, and I optimistically expected the extra bags would easily slot around their supine bodies.

It was already the beginning of July and the airless marina left our cabins on board Seahawk hot and stuffy, despite the boat's air conditioning system. Anxious to relax before the long drive ahead, and singularly determined to get a good night's rest, Jani and I barely slept a wink until just before dawn; we eventually awoke as the morning breeze began to waft its deliciously salty air through the port holes. After a meagre breakfast we began the fraught business of deciding what to cram into the car, a task that accounted for most of the day. Presents for friends and family were first to be loaded – olive oil, lemons, some of the local glassware and so on – followed in turn by a horde of toys our children could not live without for a single day. Next to be packed was a medicine case stuffed with potions and remedies for every ailment known to mankind. Finally, at Jani's insistence, several carrier bags containing enough snacks, rations and bottles of water to keep us all alive for a month – just in case we got thoroughly lost and ran out of petrol in some uncharted wilderness known only to ravenous vultures and wolves. On top of all this jumble the children's beds were made up on the back two rows of seats, with favourite bedfellows carefully placed at the ready beside each pillow.

Our departure needed to be delayed as long as possible in the hope both children might sleep soundly through the twelve hour trip. To that end we took no siesta and somehow Jani kept Miranda awake while I wrote out a summary of navigator's directions for our complicated cross-country route to Santander. (Jani and map reading were not words that belonged together in any Christian sentence.) By early evening the temperature was still in the high eighties; we longed to go inside the boat and turn on the air conditioning, but I had decommissioned everything in readiness for our five week absence from Seahawk. For supper Miranda had her fresh vegetable mush and the rest of us had crusty bread rolls from the local bakery, filled with cheese and salad, followed by fruit yoghurts, so no washing up was required. Finally, at nine o'clock it was time to leave. Both children had already fallen asleep on the cushions in the cockpit, so we carried them to the car and turned on the air conditioning. Leaving the marina and the bustle of Moraira behind us, we wound our way beneath the slopes of Montgó towards Jesús Pobre, basking in the welcome cool before we arrived at the finca to pick up our bags of new clothes.

I left Jani and the children locked in the car, as had become my habit, and quickly scouted around the outside of the building. To my intense relief I found all the latest padlocks, chains and bars on our isolated finca had remained undisturbed since the previous day. Reassured, I unlocked the gates in the archway leading to the inner courtyard, turned the keys in the heavy front door and trudged upstairs to fetch our luggage from its hiding place in the airing cupboard. It was bare. I checked through the empty rooms with quickening pulse and noticed to my horror that a tiny ventilation window, high above the landing by the children's bedroom, was wide open. Its wire mesh screen had been torn away.

I ran downstairs and out into the vineyard, still certain that no intruder could have scaled the high, featureless back wall of the house without a long and very conspicuous ladder. But there in a furrow of russet soil, barely visible in the lengthening evening shadows between the rows of grape laden vines, lay our swimming pool skimmer. The long telescopic handle had been extended to the full twelve feet of its reach, the oval leaf net roughly hacked from its metal frame. Glancing around I caught sight of a patch of trampled undergrowth, where two of our holdalls lay empty and abandoned beneath the high window. Instantly the whole thing slid into place. Rooted to the spot for a moment I invoked a fearful torrent of commination upon the heads of the heartless burglars, in the same breath cursing my own idiocy in imagining for a moment that La Abubilla was no longer under surveillance.

" Come on! Why haven't you brought anything down yet?" I heard Jani calling. "I need to get at our warm clothes for the ferry tomorrow morning."

Then more suspiciously, as she saw me from the far side of the courtyard, "What are you doing out there amongst the vines? Where *are* all our bags, anyway?"

"They're bloody-well gone! Every last stitch of clothing!", I wailed, stomping upstairs once more in disbelief. "We haven't even worn them yet! They've even taken my old gardening jeans this time ... the unspeakable bastards!"

I had already pieced the puzzle together and instantly pictured a scruffy urchin, with the metal hoop of the pool net tucked under his arms, being hoisted up the sheer wall to the window by a pair of swarthy ruffians below. After tugging away the wire mesh screen and wriggling his way sinuously through the opening, the little ragamuffin – necessarily smaller and slimmer than Rory – would have emptied our bags and thrown their contents to his accomplices below. Whether he had used a rope to make his escape afterwards, or whether he was perhaps some circus acrobat or contortionist I no longer cared.

"Let's go!" cried Jani desperately from the courtyard. "Let's just for God's sake go home!"

Closing the front door behind us, this time without bothering to lock it, we set off for Santander. A little after midnight on a lonely road in a wooded hinterland beyond Teruel, I was suddenly horrified to find twenty foot high walls of flame erupting from either side of the empty road. My expletive had been loud enough to disturb Jani from her sleep – no mean feat.

"It's suddenly got very hot in here," she complained from the pillow on her reclined seat. "Why have you turned off the air conditioning? And what's that smell? Is the engine overheating?"

"Yes it has, no I haven't, and no it isn't," I answered tetchily. "Just look outside!"

" Mmm, must be a wildfire," Jani murmured indifferently as the intense heat radiated through the windows. "Put your foot down," she added as an afterthought before sinking back into the depths of untroubled slumber.

Armageddon itself could not have diverted her from the shortest route home, even with our two children fast asleep on the back seats behind us. Our car emerged from the smoke a minute later to be met with a fleet of fire trucks racing from the opposite direction. Fortunately no burning tree had fallen across the road in front of us, or the outcome of that journey would have been very different.

Thirty-six hours later we drove off the ferry in rain-lashed Plymouth, shivering in stale summer clothes from a fiercer latitude with our collars turned up against a headwind of recrimination and a tailwind of regret.

Chapter 8 – Jani

The Last Ferry

March on. Do not tarry. To go forward is to move toward perfection.
March on, and fear not the thorns, or the sharp stones on life's path.

Kahlil Gibran

This time the burglars had taken everything we needed for our long journey back to England, including the crucial bag of warmer clothes for us all. The weather was many degrees cooler when Jeremy finally switched off the engine in Santander early the following morning. The children were shivering in their pyjamas and I knew it would be cooler still on the air conditioned ferry; moreover the climate when we disembarked in Plymouth would feel positively polar after the high temperatures to which we had become so gradually acclimatised since January. In desperation I searched the port area for a shop that wasn't selling beachwear to the tourists. Most of them hadn't yet opened, but I eventually found one displaying a lightweight tracksuit to fit Rory in purple – no other colours available – then I found a tiny identical one for Miranda in the same shade. But what about me? I only possessed the strappy sundress I was wearing. In desperation I looked at the very back of the rail for a larger one that might fit; and there in all its violet glory was yet another tracksuit to match the children's, clearly marked *Age 14*, but plenty generous enough for me. As for Jeremy, he would rather have borrowed a Morris dancer's costume complete with bells than be seen wearing a tracksuit, so he would have to make do with what he was wearing.

It was a relief to board the ferry and settle ourselves into our air conditioned cabin, where we certainly needed the tracksuits. We were all very hungry and immediately sought out the cafeteria for breakfast. Rory and I sat at a table with Miranda in her pushchair, while Jeremy went to queue at the counter. He came back with a tray laden with breakfast for us all; as he put it down on the table he sighed and rolled his eyes with exhaustion, having driven all through the night.

"I've just tried to order breakfast in four different languages," he confessed, complaining in the next breath that French waiters always made it a point of honour to affect utter bafflement whenever an Englishman attempted to converse in their tongue.

Although we had both been speaking a fair bit of Spanish for the last six months, it was always Greek that came more easily to us after our two years in Cyprus. French flowed readily enough after an initial moment of awkwardness, because we had both studied it for years at school; Jeremy had also spent a long summer beside the River Loire, studying at the *Institut Touraine* when he was seventeen – 'studies', incidentally, which mostly involved driving his motorbike to the local chateaux and vineyards. Whenever we were on the Continent, English words generally came to us only as a last resort when all other options had been exhausted. (However one waiter on the Italian island of San Pietro did manage to flummox us completely. During our honeymoon Jeremy and I had sailed into the little visited island's capital, Carloforte, and gleefully went ashore for supper. We had only been at sea for a couple of nights since leaving Menorca, but we were in the mood to see how far one of our exotic 100,000 lire banknotes would stretch; although worth less than fifty pounds, we discovered that such a large quantity of lire went a very long way. Our choice of pasta from the menu merited a decent red wine; but try as we might – the Italian word for *red* having deserted us – we could not make the waiter understand. We asked for *vin rouge, vinho tinto, kókkino krasí, rotwein, kirmizi şarap*, but none of these produced a glimmer of comprehension. Jeremy even pointed to his red sailing shorts, but all he got back was a confused *pantaloni, signore?* Eventually a waiter who wasn't dumb appeared at our table and together we alighted successfully on *rosso,* of course, *vino rosso.* The bill for our well deserved supper came to less than 12,000 lire and we came out of the restaurant with a handful of smaller banknotes in change).

I was very excited to see a cinema on this ship, with boards advertising the films to be shown during the 24-hour crossing. Rory had been desperate to see *Crocodile Dundee,* which had just arrived in English cinemas, but it had been given a 15 certificate by the British Board of Film Censors, in their wisdom, despite far less suitable films having 12 or even 'U' ratings. Imagine Rory's delight when he noticed the bill board advertising an afternoon screening of *Crocodile Dundee*; we decided to try to go in with both children, knowing Miranda would sleep through the entire showing. The cinema was free of charge and there was nobody to challenge us as we took our seats in the darkness. The film was an innocent romp, apart from the brief appearance of a bushman's knife, but the scene that had upset the delicate sensibilities of the censors was a moment where the beautiful heroine strips down to her underwear to drink from a billabong – the thong displaying her shapely bottom.

Incidentally I am still shocked to my core that the first *Harry Potter* film was rated a 'U' certificate despite one scene showing the evil villain drinking the blood of a Unicorn he has slain. Rory took me to the cinema to see the film when he was 19, having read the book when it was first published. (His first edition copy was given away to a charity shop soon afterwards ... hair is still being torn out whenever we remember that.) Sitting with her father a row in front of us was a tiny girl of about five, who had to be carried out of the auditorium screaming in unconfined terror when that gratuitously ghoulish scene appeared. In these enlightened days the films and television programmes all carry some message or other warning of flashing lights, strong language, extreme violence, or meanness to a minority group. It might be simpler to use a generic warning stating that someone somewhere will find good reason to be offended if they look hard enough.

After landing at Plymouth Docks our first port of call was my parents' house at Thurlestone, handily nearby in South Devon. They were thrilled to see us safely back in England again and had prepared the spare bedrooms for our arrival, placing a travel cot in our room for Miranda. Rory was in his element, with undivided attention from his doting grandparents, a large garden to play in without the fear of snakes or scorpions, and the beach practically on the doorstep. From my point of view I was able to relax and breathe easy again for the first time since our string of burglaries had begun in Spain all those months ago. After reading about foreigners being shot in their villas, any thought of spending another moment at La Abubilla, especially with the children, was out of the question. Naturally my parents were greatly relieved to hear we had decided to sell the finca when we returned to Spain for Rory's last term at the Lady Elizabeth. He was so happy there and it was a pity he would have to leave, but we had already enrolled him for the Spring and Summer terms at a small private school in Torquay until his time at his chosen school began.

I trawled the few small shops in Kingsbridge for some clothes for us all, which only served to remind me why we had so few regrets at leaving this town last December. Disinterested shop assistants and a dismal selection of summer clothing soon sent me scurrying back to Hoopers, the elegant and well stocked department store on The Strand in Torquay. It seemed so much longer than five years since I had produced, directed and modelled in the store's first fashion show at the Imperial Hotel to celebrate their opening. Rory had been a year old then and the assistants in the children's department who remembered him as a toddler fussed over him like a clutch of broody hens, plying him with sweets as he tried on clothes – he loved every minute.

Most of our friends lived within an hour's drive of Thurlestone and it was natural that we wanted to spend most of our holiday in Devon. But Jeremy's mother was longing to see the children again and we soon went to stay at my parents-in-law's home near Arundel for a few days. Our long drive to rural West Sussex marked the first occasion we ever stopped for supper with the children at somewhere civilised, rather than at a (long since extinct) Little Chef favoured by Rory – mainly due to the Lego table where children could play until their meals arrived. The Dorset pub we chose was unusual, if not unique, firstly because it tolerated children in its fireside bar, and secondly, since it boasted a glorious view over the sea from its terrace on the Jurassic Coast. Following this highly successful supper Miranda's first words, after the familiar *Mama, Dada, Worwy* and *more?*

more?, were PUB MEAL! PUB MEAL!, squeaked out repeatedly in her most excited voice whenever we drove anywhere, until we gave in and promised her another outing.

Liz was also delighted to hear we had abandoned our finca to its burglars; she was already plotting with my mother to view some suitable houses for us in Devon on our behalf as soon as we had returned to Spain. It was at my parents-in-law's rambling house in Sussex that we first noticed Rory's sudden reluctance to go upstairs alone, his nervousness a direct result of the numerous burglaries. This fear would plague him for a year or so, but as soon as Miranda could walk he would ask her to go upstairs with him, often pushing her gently ahead like a hostage. Luckily she was always delighted to oblige, particularly if the promise of a sweet was involved.

During that summer in England Vanessa called from Munich to invite us to share a quaint holiday cottage in Dittisham at end of August for the week of the Dartmouth Regatta. The regatta had become a keenly anticipated fixture in our lives that had rarely been missed; the formal cocktail party at our yacht club and several distinctly informal parties at our friends' fabulous houses in Kingswear were only eclipsed by the appearance of the Red Arrows, who in those days performed their wingtip acrobatics perilously low over the River Dart. Our viewing platform was usually the deck of Valdora, Jeremy's splendid classic yacht which his former partners still owned; her mooring in the middle of the river was almost directly below the flight path at the exact point at which pairs of the Hawker jet aircraft approached each other head on at phenomenal speed, before skilfully avoiding collision and catastrophe at the very last second. The guests on board, often twenty or more, were amongst a handful of privileged people who were close enough to make out the pilots' faces as the jets roared overhead.

Apart from this spectacular aerial event, Rory preferred to stay with my parents. Nevertheless when the day came to move into the holiday cottage our car was still brimful with enough baby clothes and equipment to open a branch of Mothercare. Jeremy and I were disappointed, to say the least, that the 'country cottage on the banks of the River Dart', as described by the letting agents, turned out to be a dismal 1960s bungalow covered in peeling grey render artistically decorated with streaks of verdigris. It was directly beside the road running through the village, there was not a patch of garden and it was one of the few houses in Dittisham without the slightest glimpse of the river. We hoped the bungalow would be more appealing inside, but it wasn't; the depressing, post-war utility furniture looked as if it had been scavenged from the leftovers of a house clearance sale. Stefan, Vanessa and daughter Sara had arrived before us and were busy unpacking, having chosen the larger bedroom of the two.

Jeremy and I wished we had stayed at home. I decided not to let Miranda use the grubby travel cot in our tinsel-strewn room that plainly hadn't been cleaned since Christmas; instead she could sleep in one of the singles while Jeremy and I made do. At that moment we were startled by a shriek from Vanessa. We rushed into her bedroom where she pointed a shaking finger at the double bed. I went closer to get a better look. There, on the dusty mahogany shelf above the headboard was a complete set of ten, yellowing toenail clippings, proudly displayed in order as neatly as chess pieces. I felt quite sick – it could only have been worse if there were twelve of them. The letting agency had closed for the day, so we spent an unpleasant, sleepless night imagining what other horrors might be lurking. The next morning we left as quickly as possible, not daring to use as much as a tea cup. Eventually Vanessa was given a substantial discount on the extortionate rent already paid, but to our minds she should have received compensation for a ruined holiday. It was a disappointing end to our English summer, but saying goodbye to both sets of parents was very much easier; this time they knew it would only be a matter of months before they had us back for good, and in time for Christmas.

Returning to Spain in time for the first day of Rory's school term we were told the tragic news that the eighteen year-old son of Rory's teacher had been killed in a car accident near Jávea. I was staggered to see this devoted teacher and mother already back at school, so soon after the fatal accident. A memorial service was held in the Parroquia del Mar, the Fisherman's Church built in 1967 in Duanes de la Mar, Jávea's fishing district, to which all parents were invited. What can you usefully say in such a situation? I just hugged her and told her how desperately sorry I was, but it didn't seem nearly enough. Everyone from the Lady Elizabeth came to the church; children, parents, teachers and friends of the family filled the pews of this extraordinary building. Outwardly the church has the appearance of a large fishing boat under construction, its prow pointing seawards with its ribs and planking buttressed by the heavy timber props and chocks found in a shipyard. Inside the building another surprise awaits, for the ceiling is constructed of red pine in the form of a wooden hull, which is said to symbolise St. Peter's fishing boat. The service in such a special atmosphere was all the more moving and I couldn't help wishing there had been a similar memorial for my brother Christopher after he was drowned in Torbay at the age of fifteen; that was different however, as his body was never found and my poor parents were never able to say goodbye.

Life on board Seahawk was delightful, now that the fiercest heat had gone out of the sun. Every morning before school we would ride our bikes to the bakery, collect our croissants and fresh bread and return for a quick tour around the marina. Miranda would be happily strapped into a baby seat behind Jeremy, Rory pedalled the new bike on which he had just learned to ride without stabilisers and I brought up the rear on my 'ladies shopping bicycle', thoughtfully designed by some misogynist with a large basket attached to the handlebars. For the three months of the Christmas term the weather remained perfect, pleasantly cooler than the summer yet still far warmer than Devon in July. We only needed to turn on the heating in the boat during the evenings and first thing in the morning. Each Saturday we visited the open air market and browsed the stalls, buying quantities of seedless clementines so fresh they still clung to their little leafy stems. At the fish market we bought enormous swordfish steaks, fresh off the boats that morning; they were often being cut from the whole beautiful glistening fish as we arrived – a sight I couldn't bear to witness, which was hypocritical and cowardly as I loved eating the grilled steaks. I also managed to persuade one of the fishermen to give Rory an amputated sword, which he proudly dried in the sun and brought home to England; it hung in the laundry room at our manor house for many years until we moved.

From first light local farmers, traders and gypsies would set up their stalls; the choicest fruits and vegetables glistening with the water sprinkled over them by the vendors to keep them fresh. Alongside produce from the market gardens and smallholdings jostled stalls displaying leather goods, a plethora of handbags and belts hanging enticingly from metal stands and swinging gaily in the breeze. Elsewhere convincing, real leather copies of Gucci, Chanel and Louis Vuitton accessories competed with the more traditional styles favoured by the black-clad Spanish grannies. My absolute favourite was a stall selling every conceivable variety of nut, offered loose by the kilo; each tub had a nifty little silver shovel to scoop the nuts into bags for weighing. Displayed on the table were smooth cream peeled almonds, wrinkly brown walnuts, roasted cashews with a fine crust of salt, plump peanuts with their papery skins on, and large pistachios bursting pinkly from their shells. Rory and I loved the roasted sugared almonds which came in long, slim cellophane cones twisted at the top, just like miniature furled umbrellas. The caramelised coating of these irresistible almonds was brown, sticky and tasted exactly like toffee apples.

Rory's favourite stall sold freshly made hot *Churros*, the ridged, cinnamon flavoured finger-shaped doughnuts coated in caster sugar and served with a pot of dark hot chocolate sauce in which to dip them. We could smell them frying as soon as we approached the market and, if I close my eyes, I can smell them to this day. My best efforts to keep sugar away from my children were rapidly dissolving in this land of delicious sweet treats. (They were a great novelty then; now, I am delighted to say, they are even sold in the Coastal Café at Treyarnon Bay on the North Coast of Cornwall during the summer months).

Jeremy and I needed little persuasion to sample local wines

and were delighted to be invited to a vineyard set 1500 feet up in the Sierra Bernia mountains near Parcent. Our friends Lynda and Ian had leased some of the vines and in this way became members of an exclusive club where one Sunday every month lunch was served for the members and their guests. *Bodega Maserof* was centred around a 17th century farmhouse, itself built on the site of a Roman villa, which was restored in the 1970s by an Englishman. Wine production had ceased several decades earlier when the vines succumbed to disease, but Peter successfully re-established vine cultivation on the fertile slopes of the Sierra Bernia. In September his grapes were harvested in the traditional manner and adventurous members of his club were invited to tread the grapes by foot; they would eventually receive complimentary bottles of the new vintage.

The journey into the mountains was a breath of fresh air for us; the regularity of our afternoon excursions by dinghy to the beach at El Portet, the only sheltered beach for miles, had become rather limiting. Refreshingly the warm airs of the coastal plains cooled as we climbed higher and the scents of thyme, sage and a hundred other wild herbs wafted through the open car windows. The entrance to Maserof was imposing. An ancient stone archway framed enormous oak doors that led to a roughly paved terrace surrounded by picturesque half-timbered white-washed buildings, where tables and chairs were set for lunch. Giant earthenware pots and antiquated wine barrels spilled over with vermillion geraniums; old wooden cartwheels and the relics of dusty farm implements decorated every corner. Sitting im-movably over an open fire in the middle of the terrace was the largest iron frying pan I had ever seen; it must have been four feet across and was full to the brim with gently bubbling paella, which was being lovingly stirred by an ample Spanish lady with a giant wooden spoon. Peter gathered our small group together and led us to his bodega to sample the previous year's vintage. As he handed small taster glasses to his visitors I declined, explaining that red wine always gave me headaches, particularly if drunk in the daytime.

Peter patiently explained that my headaches were due to the amount of preservatives in wine, not the alcohol. He told me that even organically grown wines often had sulphur added, although his did not. He persuaded me to sample his red wine with a promise that I would not get a headache. The wine was deliciously fruity and smooth; I was so convinced by Peter's guarantee that I abandoned all my previous convictions and several glasses slipped down easily with lunch. Rory and Carmella drank locally produced apple juice and enjoyed their children's portions of paella. Miranda sat in her pram beside our table and enjoyed the atmosphere, if not the paella; I thought its richness might upset her delicate tummy so she had her usual home-made mush with some bread. She was cutting teeth at the time and her favourite teething ring was always an olive with the stone removed, which she would worry like a puppy with a bone. There was never a shortage, wherever we went; a complimentary dish of ripe olives, a basket of crusty bread and a bottle of mineral water was always served as soon as one sat down at any restaurant in Spain. (Nowadays in England we consider ourselves fortunate to get as much as a uselessly thin, complimentary paper napkin.)

As we wound our way back down the mountain road I kept looking at my watch, waiting for the hour hand to reach four o'clock, the time my head would normally start aching after drinking red wine at lunchtime. I consoled myself that at least

I wouldn't have to cook supper as we had all eaten enough and boiled eggs and Marmite soldiers would suffice before bedtime. Five o'clock came and went with no sign of a headache, we reached home an hour after that and I was still feeling fine. By bedtime I could hardly believe my head was still clear and from that day on I determined to buy preservative free wine, although once back in 'Pudding Island' the quest proved impossible.

We decided to fly back to England for a few days at half-term; air fares were very reasonable because the English schools had a later half term. Besides, we thought it would be a good idea to visit the pre-prep school in Torquay which Rory would be joining in the New Year. We drove to Alicante airport and arrived in good time to park for our early evening departure, checking in our luggage shortly before our flight number flashed up as delayed. Jeremy inquired at the airline desk and discovered we were facing a four hour wait, as the plane was held up and hadn't even left Gatwick.

Jeremy, who detested the crowded, cigarette smoke filled airport lounges and their legions of fast food outlets, suggested we drive along the coast to find somewhere decent for an early supper; I suspected the thought of four hours worth of danger-ous duty-free shopping might also have been weighing heavily on his mind. We didn't have to drive very far before coming to an attractive little fishing retreat with a charming restaurant, thankfully quiet as it was out of the way and out of season. It was a beautiful evening, mild for October, as we took a table on a terrace overlooking the fishermen's gaily painted boats as they gently bobbed on a calm Mediterranean sea. Jeremy and I settled down to enjoy our seafood and chilled white wine, Rory attack-ing his favourite 'onion rings' and chips as Miranda demolished some mashed banana and yoghurt. We congratulated ourselves on our brilliant idea, pouring scorn on the unfortunates we had left behind to their junk food at the airport. In no particular hurry we eventually returned to the car and drove our leisurely way back along the coast to the airport car park. ('There's plenty of time, I don't expect the plane has even reached the Pyrenees yet,' my husband confidently reassured.)

The main hall was worryingly empty as Jeremy went to check the departures board. Miranda was dozing in her push-chair and I thought it might be wise to change her into her pyjamas so she could sleep undisturbed on the flight and be popped into bed as soon as we got back. I reclined the back of the push-chair and started to undress her. At the precise moment I was pulling on her pyjama bottoms, Jeremy came running (a sight rarely seen) towards us shouting and gesticulating, followed by an irate airline stewardess who was firing a stream of Spanish at us.

"Our flight left on time!" he shouted. "The crafty so and so's brought in another plane!"

I stood there agape, with a half naked baby, a shocked little boy with eyes like saucers and the seats surrounding us covered with hand luggage and an open baby bag, its contents strewn about willy-nilly.

"We might just catch the flight that's about to leave, but only IF YOU HURRY! We have to run, because it's the last plane to England tonight!"

The thought of spending the night in the lounge of some hideously expensive airport hotel with two very tired children spurred me into action. I threw a blanket over Miranda and told Rory to grab his knapsack and whatever else he could carry, stuffed the half-open baby bag under the pushchair and ran after

Jeremy who, laden like a packhorse, was already running after the stewardess towards the horizon. Rory ran after me and immediately slipped and fell on the polished marble floor, dropping everything he had managed to scoop up, all of which scattered and rolled away under the rows of chairs. I ran back to help him to his feet, spinning the unruly push-chair around so fast it almost tipped over.

"Take Rory's hand!" I yelled at my husband's back. Poor Rory looked terrified, having never before seen either of his parents in such a state of panic.

"It's all right darling," I said. "The plane won't go without us."

"Si, Señora, it most certainly will!" the sprinting stewardess shouted unhelpfully over her shoulder.

At that point I really wished she couldn't speak English. We ran on for what seemed like miles towards the farthest departure gate until one of my favourite *Alexandre of Paris* hair combs, bought eight years earlier in Harrods as part of my trousseau, fell out and bounced away over the shiny floor; I was running so fast that it landed way behind me. I started to turn the push-chair around but of course the blasted jockey wheels, perverse as a supermarket trolley, instantly swivelled in the opposite direction and locked up in a pigeon-toed pickle. Jeremy looked around and shouted at me again.

"What are you doing? Come on!"

"My hair comb's fallen out!"

"B***** the comb. Leave it or we'll miss the plane!"

I took a final glance back at the pretty peach coloured comb lying abandoned against a litter bin. Its partner was still in my hair but I was heartbroken; I had worn them with my going away outfit on my wedding day. We must have looked a spectacle as we dashed pell mell through empty corridors to the very farthest departure gate, Miranda's pushchair easily mistaken for one of *Ben Hur's* chariots – the nearest departure lounges at any airport, in case you wondered, are only there for show and are in fact holograms or nicely executed trompe l'oeil paintings. Somehow we made it in the nick of time and flopped exhaustedly into our seats, as two hundred fellow passengers scowled and tutted at us derisively. The aircraft was in the air before we had even fastened our seatbelts.

For once in my life I sat in stony silence all the way back to England, mourning my lost hair comb as Rory and Miranda fell peacefully asleep. Jeremy was unsympathetic. He had never liked those gold wire inlaid, peachy pink hair combs, which he called my 'wired gums', as they reminded him of a set of toothless dentures. Nice! He was also smarting about his flight miscalculation: it was due entirely, he insisted, to the way the cunning airline had so sneakily commandeered a replacement aircraft. Besides, he complained, our original flight had taken off illegally with our luggage, but without us; as such he was convinced the airline was duty bound to take us on any later flight, even if we had decided to pitch a tent and stop for a leisurely champagne breakfast on the boarding gangway.

A week later during the English half term holiday our Salcombe friends came to stay at their parents' villa in Moraira. We spent most days together and Rory was delighted to have his old friend Katherine to play with again. We enjoyed long lunches at the local fish restaurants, forays into the mountains, leisurely days on Seahawk and picnics at El Portet.

Before the less reliable winter weather set in, we decided to have an early supper at *Los Amigos del Montgó* while the evenings were still warm enough to sit out on the terrace. Conveniently situated on the Jesús Pobre road, about five kilometres inland from Jávea, the restaurant sheltered under the shadow of Monte Montgó. The attractive architecture was typical of the area, mellow pinky golden stone archways, terraces and pretty balustrades surrounded the large terrace. Flowering plants trailed and tumbled in abundance and traditional Spanish lanterns interspersed with ropes of white fairy lights lent the whole place the air of a fiesta. The menu was so extensive it could easily take half an hour to make a decision, a process luxuriously extended by the delicious tapas, crudités and dainty slices of toasted bread to dip in the rich *Alioli*, as the Catalans call it. This moorish mixture of home made mayonnaise, crushed garlic, olive oil and touch of lemon juice was a particular favourite I copied many times. Of course the garlic was fresh and the huge lemons were picked from the trees growing in the restaurant's garden and I too had been so lucky to have juicy lemons growing on our own land. As we now considered ourselves locals rather than tourists, we ordered the whole meal in our best Spanish, Rory chipping in to ask for his favourite *unos calamares con patatas fritas por favor* with a perfect accent.

Our young waiter was charming, patiently writing our complicated order on his notepad; a good looking boy of about 20, he was dressed in the obligatory crisp white shirt, the cuffs neatly rolled back a couple of times to show off his well formed sun tanned arms, and unbelievably tight, shiny black trousers. Miranda had always shown an irresistible fondness for Spanish waiters and smiled her special, gap-toothed smile at him. We never understood *exactly* why she was so obsessed with these young men; could it be the jet black, slicked back, glossy hair or the flashing white teeth? It couldn't yet be the seductive, sultry brown eyes, with heavy eyelids permanently at half mast and fringed with thick black lashes, which AV had called 'Bedroom Eyes' to her teenage protégées – hopefully it would be another eighteen years before she succumbed to those. They would affectionately murmur *Ah, la rubia* (Hello little blondie) as they bent low to reach her tiny ear. We decided it was more likely that whenever they saw her peaches and cream complexion and white blonde curls as she sat up like a little princess in her pram, they couldn't resist patting her hair or gently pinching her cheek.

She was accustomed to this doting, but that evening she had obviously determined to return the compliment at the first opportunity. Just as our waiter leant over to pour Jeremy's wine, his back to the rest of us, Miranda reached out and grabbed his tempting black trousered bottom in her little fist, giving it an affectionate squeeze. With a gasp of shock, he slopped the wine onto the tablecloth, shot *me* an accusing glance and rushed off into the kitchens, blushing with acute embarrassment. We heard great guffaws of laughter from within as all seven staff assembled to peer out of the doorway to get a good look at this brazen English hussey. Amidst much goading and lewd jibes from his colleagues our waiter returned to our table, whereupon I hurriedly explained that it wasn't me but my baby daughter; he nodded politely but I noticed he studiously kept his distance from my chair for the remainder of the evening.

Early in December the Lady Elizabeth was arranging a Nativity Play and carol service in the Fisherman's Church. The younger children were asked to come as 'Children from Foreign Lands' and I racked my brains to think of a suitable costume. Rory's best friend in his class was now a girl called Samantha, whose angelic looks derived from a Chinese mother and an English father; her mother's task was easy, as Samantha already had embroidered satin Chinese pyjamas. My English friend Lynda was good at sewing and had made Carmella a pretty blue and white Dutch milkmaid's outfit, complete with tiny white cap – with her blonde pigtails she looked perfect. I am even worse at needlework than cooking, so with absolutely no sewing equipment, I realised I would have to be inventive. I wished either of Rory's grandmothers were with us, both of them being excellent seamstresses. Mummy used to make my long evening dresses in the 'seventies and Liz had made costumes for the Ballet Rambert when she was expecting Jeremy and, much later, for her ballet school at the farm. One thing I did have on Seahawk – goodness knows why – was a silky white turban; I used to wear it in the 1970s to go to modelling assignments as it kept my curly hair perfectly straight when tucked up inside it, even if the weather was damp. Aladdin sprang to mind, but I would need to invent some baggy Turkish pantaloons. Rummaging in the crew cabin I found a very old duvet cover that looked vaguely Levantine with its delicate pattern of dark pink on a white background. I folded it in half, laid it on the carpet in the saloon and drew the outline of the pants with a felt tipped marker pen. When it was cut out I pinned the halves together and asked Rory to try the hareem pants on. After a few tucks here and there, they seemed to fit and looked quite effective.

I had no sewing machine, although Jeremy had often threatened to buy me one for Christmas – I would rather have been given a set of drain rods – but then I had a brilliant idea. Borrowing Jeremy's stapler I stapled all the seams together, hand sewing elastic into the hems of the legs. The waist could be covered with a wide pink silk scarf of mine and tied as a cummerbund to fit Rory's tiny middle; he could wear his white school shirt and I found another pink silk scarf to wrap around the shirt to look like a bolero. I added a few bits of costume jewellery and some sequins to the turban and was quietly delighted with the resulting costume. A pair of red velvet slippers could easily pass for Arabian footwear after I had glued two red pom-poms on each toe. I tucked a plastic dagger into the sash, instructing Rory that he was not to remove it and start terrorising his fellow pupils. Sitting in the church with the other parents, I watched with pride and joy as Rory's class made their way in pairs down the centre aisle towards the temporary stage. But Rory was walking in the most peculiar way, almost as if he was a bandy-legged cowboy who had just dismounted. After the children from foreign lands had laid all their gifts at baby Jesus' manger, the children came back to take their seats with the rest of the congregation. Sitting next to Samantha, Rory was in front of us so I whispered to ask him why he was walking so awkwardly. He frowned at me over the back of his pew.

"It's all the staples," he said. "They're cutting my legs!"

19th November 2024

Dear Louise,

With compliments

Thank you very much for your order

All good wishes, Jani

www.themanorhousestories.com

www.janitullychaplin.com/books

Chapter 9 – Jeremy

Hasta la Vista

There's nothing like a jolly good disaster to get people to start doing something.

His Majesty King Charles III

Bound for Spain again at the end of August the four of us returned to live on board Seahawk in the safety of the marina until it was time to return home to Devon for good at Christmas. It was an excellent season to be on the boat again; the sea was at its hottest, the sun shone for us every day and we would be jolly unlucky if we saw more than three days of rain during those months before Christmas. At weekends we could easily potter from the marina in Seahawk's tender to the little visited beach at El Portet at the drop of a hat. We all slept remarkably well in our plush cabins; as the sea air floated through the port holes and the hull rocked imperceptibly, deep sleep was nigh on impossible to resist. In all honesty Seahawk was better equipped, more comfortable and certainly easier to maintain than our finca. With no pool, garden or vineyard to worry about, it occurred to me that I should have considered buying a much larger boat and doing without any property ashore when we had first moved to Spain. At least we wouldn't have been robbed to distraction.

Pepe the chief *marinero* was delighted to see us living permanently on board Seahawk, as it gave him the chance to chat at every opportunity, day or night. 'Chapleen!' he would call as he stood at the end of our gangway with the remains of a bocadillo and in one hand and a sheaf of letters in the other. 'I have the mail for you: an electricity bill and two letters from England today!' It had given me quite a jolt the first time he bellowed 'Chapleen!' across the car park, convinced for one stomach churning moment that I was back at prep school, summoned once more for the cane. Pepe must have got in a tangle with my name as it appeared on letters from home – Christian name before surname being the opposite of the Spanish order – and I never had the heart to correct his mistake. As far as he was concerned I was Mr Chaplin Jeremy.

If our sabbatical had not exactly lived up to our highest expectations, we were still enjoying life in our sunny corner of Spain. We made the most of it, knowing too well that our footloose days would soon be curtailed by the rigid calendar of school terms, by the small matter of earning a living and by the necessary acceptance that it was time to put on some sensible shoes. In the meantime we had to sell La Abubilla.

I was still racking my brain for any reason why our perfect little finca had been singled out as a training ground for up-and-coming burglars, when the majority of isolated rural properties in the area had never lost as much as a watering can. We had since learnt that Maria, our flapdusting maid upon whom suspicion had so easily fallen, was distantly related to Spitting Manuel. Several generations ago a member of their family had owned our finca as well as other parcels of land in the valley; perhaps the old Napoleonic laws of inheritance had left a bitter taste for whomever had been cheated when the properties were divided. Whatever the underlying cause of our misfortune, we would have to own up to our string of robberies when any potential buyer was eventually found for the finca.

The advertisement for La Abubilla was published in the local newspaper on the first Friday of September. The wording was much as it had appeared when we first came across it nine months earlier; only the asking price differed. By the end of that weekend the obliging receptionists at the marina office had fielded dozens of enquiries on our behalf, all of which were enthusiastically delivered by Pepe. ('Chapleen! You have another message waiting in the telephone.') Much encouraged by the response, I arranged a succession of open days at the finca for the following week.

Bank interest rates in Spain had been rising quite sharply since our arrival and the housing market was generally considered to be heading for a fall. Bargain hunters were already sniffing for blood as owners burdened with large mortgages were compelled to sell. Our situation was different and we decided to 'fly a kite', adding a substantial slice of profit to the price we had paid for our unusual finca; with luck any gain would cover the considerable expenses caused by our robbers.

The main disadvantage of selling your own property, rather than using an agent, is that you have to deal directly with the people coming to view it. You didn't need to be the greatest judge of character to identify a genuinely interested party and, as I discovered to my cost, such people were in short supply. Instead the Costa Blanca threw up more than its fair share of chancers, every other one of whom made a beeline for La Abubilla. Overbearing to the point of downright threatening, along came these jokers in their droves, the first of them setting the gold standard for those who followed. The opening tactic was always the tight lipped, inscrutable approach. Nobody had ever visited our finca without falling for its picturesque charms, even if it wasn't their particular cup of tea; but our first viewer and his sidekick (that type invariably had one) cast their disdainful sunglasses over our home as if they were inspecting a sewage treatment works.

Leaving the flunkey to guard his blacked-out BMW, the fellow produced a miniature tape recorder from a trouser pocket and began dictating the first of many comments in slow and deliberate fashion – mainly, one suspected, for my benefit. *Old farmhouse in orchard ... small ... no sea views ... no garage.* Pearls before swine, I thought as I led him from the rear courtyard into the kitchen. The device was again raised to his mouth as he scowled at the traditional latticework cupboards and stone sink, where a line of ants had resumed their defiant patrols around its rim in our prolonged absence. *Needs new kitchen ... five grand minimum.* Much the same reaction to the bathroom followed. Inspecting the airy, characterful casita with its central chimney, apex roof and lovingly grouted stone walls, his opinion was damning: *Demolition job, might get a nice double garage out of it,* he dictated smugly. Ignoring our pristine, charmingly unpretentious swimming pool, which had never lost as much as a thimbleful of water to a leak, his verdict was a simple *old pool needs digging out.* This I had already anticipated, suspecting he and his ilk would prefer something far more elaborate.

As the tour came its conclusion he summed up his observations with a further list of damning pronouncements: *full rewire ... new marble floors ... proper modern staircase; ... double glazing all round ... rip out old wooden balcony and replace with low maintenance conservatory.* I ushered him out towards his waiting car as he cagily wrote a figure in biro on the palm of his hand – the well-worn device of many a shady secondhand car dealer – and showed it to his sidekick, who smirked and nodded in agreement. Squaring himself in front of me, he opened the palm of his hand to reveal his scrawled offer indicating half our asking price, which he strongly suggested I accept before demand collapsed entirely and I became stuck in Spain for good. His clients would need to throw a lot of money at La Abubilla; after all, the property lacked a games room, a sauna, a jacuzzi and a satellite dish the size of Goonhilly Earth Station in order to watch Match of the Day.

I thanked him for wasting so much of his time with me and gently pointed out that our asking price included everything the property had to offer, rather than all the features – such as helipad, gymnasium, wine cellar and nuclear bunker – that it so sorely lacked. As the car reversed onto the track I noticed its front and rear number plates didn't match.

Chancers such as he could hold up a cracked mirror to any property, skillfully undermining the value with the practiced eye of a pawnbroker. Some of these jokers were more persistent in their quest for a bargain and even managed to track us down at the marina. Seeing Seahawk, their interest would turn on a sixpence and the whole rigmarole would begin again with a menacing *'How much for the boat, guvner? Go on then! I've got a mate who'll take it off yer hands'*. That every one of these scavenging, latter-day barrow boys were our own countrymen was a depressing indictment of British expat life on the Costa Blanca; they were up to every trick, living incognito, leaving no footprints and always staying one step ahead of the law. I began to wish we had asked an estate agent to sell the finca for us.

Of course there was genuine interest as well, but most of these decent folk baulked at the idea of buying a property boasting such an admirable record of burglaries. And who could blame them. The flow of interest had reduced to a trickle when a timely introduction was made through a mutual acquaintance. They were an English couple in their late fifties – positively old, we thought at the time – who had lived in Dénia for eight years and were already aware of our misfortunes. As soon as they saw La Abubilla they were smitten, just as Jani an I had been, and assured us they knew how to deal with our 'vagrant' problems. They planned to erect high double chainlink fences around the entire perimeter to deter future robberies; electric gates, a noisy guard dog and security lights would ensure their peace of mind. Elsewhere we had noticed many villas that were entirely enclosed by these unsightly fences; we had often wondered how anyone could bear to live within what was effectively a large tennis court at best and a prison at worst. Jani and I could never have contemplated such an eyesore in the midst of our valley of orchards, whatever the benefits, any more than we would have erected a Dutch barn on our land in Devon.

Late in November the twists and turns of the Spanish property transfer system were eventually straightened out at the local notary's office, and with several eagerly scribbled signatures on the the *escritura* we were free; it was a long awaited moment of relief. More by luck than judgement we had also come out of our little venture with enough profit to cover the expenses of everything our time in Spain had thrown at us. Not everyone would be so lucky: hard times were about to hit the overdeveloped coasts of Spain.

Several months later, back in Devon, we heard some horrifying news. True to their word the new owners of La Abubilla had erected their fences around the property. As if to prove a point the burglars had soon struck again, shooting their pet labrador dead and making off with everything of value. It made our blood run cold. Recalling the policeman's advice given to me in Gata five months earlier, we understood how extremely fortunate we had been. There was little consolation to be gained from the revelation that the finca itself had been the target, rather than my family.

To fully disentangle ourselves from Spain we needed to sell Seahawk and her mooring in Moraira, both having served their purposes. Neither of these sales could be contemplated before Christmas, nevertheless I asked Pepe the marinero if there was a waiting list for berths in the marina. There was, and he suggested an advertisement on his office noticeboard would bring speedy results. (*'Chapleen,* you can ask whatever you want!', he assured me). As promised I was soon deluged with offers from owners of gin gazebos and gladioli lovers everywhere; the berth was sold for a very satisfactory price and Seahawk was moved to a visitors' mooring where it would remain until sold. I was excessively pleased with myself for prophesying the increasing demand for moorings in the Mediterranean, but my balloon was well and truly pricked in familiar fashion. If I was so jolly clever, my father let it be known, why hadn't I bought a second marina berth in Jani's name?

Seahawk would be a harder sell, as boats always are, and as my father was undoubtedly hoping; but gently rising stock markets had recently been volatile enough for profits to be taken by the lucky few who could afford to gamble. Power boats from the better English builders such as ours were at a premium in the Mediterranean, largely because delivery costs from England on the deck of a freighter were colossal; moreover nobody was idiotic enough to contemplate the long trip across Biscay in an unfamiliar boat.

Out of the blue came a letter from the man who had missed the chance to buy Seahawk a year earlier, when I had managed to get in first. Somehow he knew of our situation and, far from hoping to take advantage of our changed plans, he wondered if I would be prepared to deliver Seahawk to Mallorca in exchange for my full asking price; it all sounded highly unlikely, but the money was wired to our account the day after the contented new owner had flown over to meet me. It was not until early in the New Year that I eventually found time to fly back to Spain, setting off for Pollensa the following day and handing Seahawk to its new owner the same evening. After our long run of bad luck I felt this stroke of good fortune was well and truly deserved.

Basking in the afterglow of our successful transactions, we decided we should climb Montgó, the local mountain resembling the head of an elephant that rises 2,500 feet in majestic isolation over the coastline between Jávea and Dénia. This sleeping giant had always seemed to be watching over us when we first moved into La Abubilla. Now, after all our robberies, I was keen to stand on top of the unobservant pachyderm's head like an angry mahout and give it a jolly good scolding for casting a blind eye over our valley. The climb was also a rite of passage of sorts which Jani, Rory and I were keen to complete, if only to take in the glorious views that reached as far as Ibiza in clear weather. The ascent, I had so foolishly imagined, would be a final coda to our chaotic time in Spain.

One diamond clear autumn day we duly began our assault, having parked on the grassy plateau at the foot of the slope. Miranda had been left with our Salcombe friend Sue and her own toddler Edward, the three of them enjoying a picnic in a secluded spot some way from our car. Sue's daughter Katherine joined us for the climb and the four of us were soon picking our way up the rocky goat track. An hour later we stood breathlessly on the dizzying summit, quietly absorbing a spectacular panorama over the dividing ribbon of coastline as it threaded its way southwards between the sapphire Mediterranean and the deceptively uniform carpets of groves, dashed here and there with clusters of new developments, whitewashed villages and dusty, rustic settlements. Directly below we could also pick out the sun glinting on the roof of our white car, almost two thousand feet below us. It was parked in splendid isolation on a bare patch of ground, less than a hundred yards from where we had left Sue and the little ones comfortably sitting on a rug beneath the shade of a cluster of stunted pines.

Then our attention was abruptly diverted from the wide horizons before us; instead Rory's sharp young eyes had caught sight of a van approaching our lonely car along the track. As if in slow motion we watched incredulously as the ant-like figure of its driver got out and proceeded with effortless ease to break open a door of our distant, matchbox car. We all shouted ourselves hoarse as the gusting thermals snatched each redoubled warning of terrible vengeance and violent retribution from our lips, but of course he heard not the faintest whisper from above, even if he had guessed where we were. Instead of scuttling off, the thief made several return journeys to our car before satisfying himself he had got all he wanted. As he ambled back to his van for the last time I could have sworn the miscreant looked up towards the peak high above him and waved his appreciation to us. Having barely caught our breath, and before giving ourselves the chance to plant a flag, I was suddenly anxious to see if our valuables had been taken from their hiding place in a recess beneath the middle row of seats.

Ascending the winding path to the summit had been exhausting enough, although Rory and Katherine had streaked away ahead of us, tackling the steepest ascents beside yawning chasms as sure-footedly as mountain goats, with a casual disregard for their own safety that I remembered from my own childhood. The descent was a great deal more demanding, taxing muscles Jani and I had long since forgotten we possessed, but after what seemed like a marathon we were back on the plateau beside our car. Damage around a window showed marks where a coat hanger had been inserted to fish for the door lock. Our bags of shopping and every single item that wasn't bolted to the car's interior had vanished: tools, fire extinguisher, umbrellas, spare bulbs and travel sweets, if not Miranda's travel potty. But there, untouched in the secret cubbyhole lay my wallet. That, at least, felt like a small victory. Sue had seen and heard nothing of the drive-by thief, which was probably the only other blessing of the day.

"Let's go home," said Jani despondently as we drove away, neither for the first nor the last time in our lives.

Chapter 10 – Jani
There's No Place Like Home.

No matter how hard the past is, you can always begin again.

Buddha

One year less a day since the carefree outset of our sabbatical we began our final overnight drive from Moraira to Santander, where the ferry to Plymouth awaited us. As we approached the port, dog tired and red eyed from the long journey, Jeremy quickly noticed the familiar outline of our ferry's tall superstructure and funnel was nowhere to be seen. A full gale from the northwest was sending a strong surge into the harbour, but beyond the mouth of the Ria enormous rollers were piling up dangerously over the shoaling seabed. Jeremy assumed our ship was delayed on its passage through Biscay, however the lady in the ticket office had far more disagreeable news for us. Our usual ferry, the smart, recently launched *Quiberon* was in dry dock and had been replaced by an aged, unstabilised tub, barely the size of the Isle of Wight ferry, which was straining against her hawsers at the quayside as we drove onto her car deck.

"We're NOT staying in this cabin!" I told Jeremy as he dumped our overnight bags onto one of the beds. "Just look at that leaking window!"

The space between the glass and the storm plate of one of our cabin windows had turned into a fish tank, half full of dirty water that was slopping lazily back and forth with the ship's slight movement even before we left harbour. How much more water would find its way in when we put to sea and, I added angrily, if that much water was trapped behind the window, how much more could there be in the ship's bilges? I wanted Jeremy to summon a steward and demand another cabin.

"Don't worry about it," he said as usual. "It's perfectly normal in a ship as old as this. I expect all the cabins are much the same and this is one of the best."

If that was supposed to console me, it didn't. I already knew I would be awake all night waiting for water to seep under the cabin door, followed by a shrill announcement to abandon ship. My vivid imagination needed no assistance from the story of *Titanic*. (Unfortunately I had seen *The Poseidon Adventure*).

A little before midday the game little ship put to sea and turned her rusty nose into the horizontal spume of a thoroughly nasty December storm, her hull complaining noisily beneath us at each encounter with the yawning troughs ahead. Our cabin was high up, directly under the bridge, where our fish tank window faced directly over the ship's bows. The ship soon began to dig her bow into the troughs as the ocean swell increased, sending walls of green water crashing directly against our cabin. Bottles and crockery clattered and smashed noisily in the restaurant beneath us with each pitch and roll of the ship. Nevertheless, as the leaking window squirted jets of seawater around our cabin and the toilet gurgled ominously like a fumarole, Jeremy and I happily abandoned Spain for the mountainous seas of Biscay without a backward glance. Jeremy strapped Miranda's travel cot to the table between our beds with a couple of leather belts while I stuffed some towels around the window frame before collapsing onto our beds.

As darkness fell over Biscay Jeremy ventured along the empty corridors in search of sustenance, but the restaurant, the bar and even the stairways were roped off. My husband has always been one of those infuriating people who never succumbs to seasickness, and he was very annoyed to find the ship's catering crew had all gone to earth; there was neither a drop nor a morsel to be found. After picking over the last scraps of stale snacks from the car, my husband surrendered to a deep and well deserved sleep after his long night's drive. All night I tossed and turned almost as much as the ship, still feeling very seasick until a grey dawn eventually broke over quieter seas off Ushant. I told Jeremy he would have to take the children for breakfast as I couldn't leave my bed. He was as surprised that I had felt so ill, never having had a moment of seasickness on our 3,000 mile honeymoon voyage to Cyprus, nor even on Seahawk, whose ability to roll about at anchor made us yearn for another catamaran. Later in the day I felt slightly better and decided to start packing our things in eager anticipation of the moment we could to get off the elderly ship. Jeremy had taken the children for lunch but came back without Rory.

"Where is he? Why on earth did you leave him?" I asked in a panic.

"He's fine, he's in the children's playroom just at the end of this corridor," he answered. "He's busy playing with some other children and he knows the way back to our cabin."

A few minutes later the door flew open and Rory rushed in, hand in hand with a beautiful dark haired, olive skinned little girl of his own age.

"This is Isabella," he announced as we stood there with our mouths open in surprise.

"She's Spanish and she doesn't speak English."

With that he sat her on his bunk and they chatted away happily in her language, which was too fast for me to follow. Jeremy and I looked at each other, deciding what to do next. Surely her parents would be wondering where she was. We put the question to Rory, who shrugged it off with a child's artlessness.

"They're still having lunch. They know where we are and I'll take her back later on."

We still felt awkward but neither child was the least bit concerned. An hour later as we were nearing Plymouth we gently suggested it was time for Rory to say goodbye and return Isabella to her family. This episode was an eye-opener to Jeremy and me, a timely portent of parental responsibilities ahead.

As soon as we arrived at my parents home in Thurlestone I telephoned our estate agent friend in Totnes; Dick had been most helpful with the marketing of our home and land beside the Salcombe estuary barely a year earlier and it was he who had given us the confidence to set the asking price extravagantly high. I explained we had just returned from Spain and were looking for a new home in South Devon, close enough for Rory to attend his new school as a day boy the following year. The lengths to which my mother and Liz had gone to find us a suitable house had been fruitless; Jeremy and I wouldn't have touched any of their choices with a bargepole – our tastes and budgets having hit a generational impasse. Dick told me he knew of a house that he thought would be ideal for us, but it wouldn't be been coming onto the market until the finishing touches to the building work had been completed. I asked if he could arrange for us to view it as soon as possible, knowing that Jeremy would be only too pleased to step in where the builders had left off.

Dick must have waved his magic wand and the following day we found ourselves driving off the beaten track to the pretty village of Broadhempston.

Emerging from the narrow twisting lane into the village, the recently converted barn was directly in front of us as we reached the bottom of the hill. *Orchard House* was painted on a pretty sign on the five-bar gate leading into the garden. Dick was waiting to show us around the L-shaped house, which was blessed with unusually well proportioned reception rooms into which light streamed; it had been too long since we had breathed in the welcome smells of fresh paint and new carpets. With five bedrooms, three bathrooms, reception rooms and a very large kitchen leading into a laundry room with a door into a spacious garden, it was perfect for us. Best of all the barn was loosely surrounded by other village houses, which was exactly what I craved after our experiences with the Spanish burglaries. Here the children and I would be reassured by the comforting glow from windows flickering through the trees around us at night, something we had not experienced at any of our previous homes. The presence of neighbours within a half-mile would be a novel experience for Jeremy, who quickly made it his mission to plant tall hedges around the entire gardens.

We completed the purchase a couple of weeks later in record time, after much solicitor badgering by Jeremy. As it happened, our lawyer's office was directly over the road from the vendor's representatives in Torquay, so we gaily imagined this proximity would speed things up. Not a bit of it. Jeremy was incandescent when he discovered the two legal firms were corresponding by letter delivered by Royal Mail, which meant a delay of three or sometimes five days between replies to run-of-the-mill queries.

He threatened to drive over, physically remove and personally deliver the correspondence unless it was walked over the road by a secretary the moment the envelope had been sealed. Time equals money as far as solicitors are concerned, and the more delay the better.

My parents helped us unpack our furniture that had arrived in two enormous removal lorries. Astonishingly we found a place for everything in our new home; even our sofas and other pieces bought in Valencia for the finca looked as if they had always been there. Ancient church pews formed an eating area at the far end of the kitchen and our antique, tile-inlaid dining table, salvaged from La Abubilla, fitted perfectly. There were however several glaring and sorely missed omissions when everything had been unpacked from Sussex. A year earlier Jeremy had stored many of our belongings in the studio at his parents' house. This long, elegant room connecting the two wings of the house had been built with a polished beech, sprung floor for Liz, who in her seventies was still much in demand as a choreographer on both sides of the Atlantic. One end of its vaulted, sixty-foot length was used on high days as a dining room and was home to a fine Sheraton dining table, (useless to man or beast because nothing could ever be safely put on it). The rest of the room, although scattered with other antique pieces, was made over to a ballet studio with an array of large, gilt framed French mirrors along the rear wall. It was at the farther end of this room that Jeremy had neatly piled the more perishable of our furniture and rails of clothes behind several panelled screens.

Predictably my father-in-law took exception to this hostile invasion of his home – which had been featured in several glossy magazines – somehow forgetting it had been designed and largely paid for by Liz; that he graced the studio with his fleeting presence fewer than five times a year was detail he had also overlooked. Summoning up a rare surge of vigour he decided to move all our belongings into a decrepit former generator house plagued with vermin and a leaking roof. Hence all our soft furnishings had become mouse fodder during our time in Spain and my best clothes, including the beautiful full length cream cashmere coat I had worn for Miranda's christening, had all but rotted into compost. It was unforgivable of him, as my mother-in-law heartily agreed.

A few hundred yards along the lane from our new home was a working dairy farm and the children and I enjoyed walking to watch the cows over the farm gate. At the top of the village was a traditional pub next door to a tiny cottage that housed a miniscule sub-Post Office and shop, in front of which was a grassy paddock with a small playpark for the local children. It wasn't long before we discovered that our cheerful Postmistress, Marlene, (a name we thought wonderfully exotic for a Devon Postmistress), cooked a large gammon joint coated in local honey every evening in her AGA and sold it sliced by hand in the shop; it was the best ham we had ever tasted. Vegetables and fruit in season, all from nearby farms or smallholdings, were supplemented with cakes, jams, marmalades, chutneys and other preserves made by ladies in the village. Every time I went into the crammed little shop Marlene would ask the same 'How are you settling in' question, which was very sweet of her, but it became rather repetitive by the time we had been in the house for two years; she would probably be enquiring three decades later, safe in the knowledge that we were still newcomers. One early morning I was walking Miranda in her pushchair to the baby and toddler playgroup in the village hall when a voice called out tentatively from behind a hedge.

"Jani?"

I swung around to see one of my oldest friends from schooldays – Jill had no idea we had moved into the village as we had lost touch over the years since leaving school. We had been in the same class at our very first school near Goodrington, then met again at Pony Club and later at Stover School as horse mad fourth formers.

"Where are you going?" she asked. When I told her she came with me and introduced me to some of the mothers she knew.

"Come and have coffee when you've finished here," she said as she left the hall.

How nice to have an old friend in the village, I thought; it was even better that Jill had more horses and ponies for her three children than she could exercise herself and asked me to hack out with her. The following day I met another neighbour who lived in a large Georgian house opposite Orchard House, extraordinarily Anna's husband David was an old friend of mine from when I briefly lived in London and my parents had been friends of his parents who lived opposite Compton Castle. Anna and David had a little girl, Amy, who was the same age as Miranda, so this would be perfect and I looked forward to the girls playing together. Another couple next door to Anna had a boy the same age as Rory; Charlie would be starting at Wolborough Hill with Rory the following year when they were seven. Broadhempston was turning out to be the best place we could have found to live and within a few weeks we had all settled in and decided the time had come to have a dog again.

Rory was going on a Saturday hack with a little riding school nearby and within a month Miranda joined him, led by me on foot. Each time we had dropped Rory at the farm, Miranda would cry because she desperately wanted to go too. Eventually Margaret, the owner of the farm, suggested we let Miranda join in, providing I could lead her on the quietest pony they owned. She took to riding like a duck to water and was soon given the nickname 'Superglue bottom' by the girls at the stables because she never fell off.

It had been a joint decision to look for a Cavalier King Charles Spaniel puppy; we had both loved Jeremy's first Cavalier, Oliver, and the breed had the reputation for being wonderful with children. Jeremy soon found an advertisement in the local paper for Cavalier puppies for sale in the next village. We took the children and were shown into the sitting room where the breeder said she would bring in a puppy. The children and I sat on the floor as two of the prettiest eight week-old Blenheim puppies imaginable came trotting enthusiastically across the carpet as if they had just jumped off the cover of a chocolate box.

'Blenheim' refers to the chestnut and white colouring of Cavalier King Charles Spaniels, adopted after the first Duke of Marlborough kept chestnut and white King Charles Spaniels for hunting (biscuits, obviously) at Blenheim Palace. They can be seen in the family portraits hanging in the Palace's Red Drawing Room. Thereafter the Duchess of Marlborough continued to breed spaniels with this Blenheim colouring.

We had not been expecting two, but the cunning breeder told us these brothers were the last of the litter and suggested we choose between them. Of course she knew jolly well that was never going to happen! One puppy went straight to Rory and climbed onto his lap as the second made a beeline for Miranda.

Jeremy got out his cheque book with a resigned sigh and we came home with both puppies. From that day on Miranda spent more time sitting in the puppies' basket with them in the kitchen than anywhere else.

Bramble and Briar filled our lives with joy; they were the most adorable puppies but very different in character, despite being brothers. Bramble was adventurous and independent, very much a boy, whereas Briar had such a feminine side he should have been a girl. Miranda put Briar in her lilac dolls' pram, dressed him in a baby bonnet and shawl and pushed him around the house and garden. He adored it and from that moment he decided the pram was his personal property and jumped into it to sleep whenever he could.

(That pram had to come with us, for Briar's sake, when we moved to our manor house when Miranda was three, and again when we moved to our farmhouse on Dartmoor eight years later. One day Jeremy decided it was just too filthy to be redeemed and had to be thrown away. I had been out that day and came home to find Briar wandering round and round the kitchen whining pathetically. Bramble, almost as selectively deaf as my husband, was fast asleep in the basket and pleased to ignore his brother's plight entirely. I accused Jeremy, who readily admitted he had taken the pram to the recycling dump in Newton Abbot. I grabbed the car keys and drove straight to the recycling centre, where I spotted the pram within minutes, paid my two pounds and brought it home to the kitchen. If a Cavalier could laugh, Briar was laughing as he leapt into the pram. It remained his favourite spot for the rest of his life. Even when he was over fourteen he could still jump into it.).

One day I became aware that the house was suspiciously quiet;

neither Miranda nor the dogs were anywhere to be seen. The garden was entirely secure, so I knew she was around somewhere and called out for her.

"I'm in the utilly room," came the reply. Along with some of her other alternative versions of words she charmingly mispronounced were the cajuzzi, Farmer Christmas, Anthony-Wrinkle cream, the boiler (sauna), dressing ground (gown) and Jofish, (Joseph of Technicolour Dreamcoat fame, her favourite baby doll given by my parents for her second Christmas.)

I found Miranda kneeling in front of the tumble drier, out of which the inquisitive heads of Bramble and Briar peered patiently out of the open door.

"They like it because it's still nice and warm," explained Miranda, who had also placed a doggie towel and a bowl of water inside the drum. I called Jeremy to take a photograph.

"Thank goodness she doesn't know how to turn it on!" he said, making a note to unplug the machine at the socket after each use.

Miranda and Briar were inseparable for fourteen and a half years. When she was three her favourite companion needed to have a broken tooth removed under anaesthetic and of course Miranda insisted on accompanying Briar into the operating room; luckily our vet John was an old family friend, who always asked Miranda to act as a surprisingly able veterinary assistant during minor procedures on either of our dogs. But on this occasion she had been horrified when preparations were made for the insertion of the cannula into a vein in his leg. 'I'll have to shave a bit off,' John explained as he held up one of Briar's front legs and inspected it.

"NO-O-O!" wailed Miranda, imagining her pet dog hobbling

along with one shortened leg forever after – probably with a crutch. She calmed down when John showed her the electric hair clippers in his other hand. Children can be so literal.

They can also be very callous. Miranda must have been four years old when our third cavalier puppy arrived. No bigger than a guinea pig, little Burberry must have wriggled in Miranda's arms as she picked him up for the first time, whereupon he fell out of her gentle grip onto the kitchen floor and landed heavily on his head. He was initially stunned by the impact and of course Miranda was desperately upset, fleeing in tears to her bedroom before the little puppy fully recovered his senses. Rory had been equally upset, but he was also a little angry with his sister. Marching upstairs after her, he told Miranda that she had killed the puppy stone dead and that Daddy had thrown him away in the dustbin. It took some time before tranquility was restored.

Rory was very happy at The Abbey and immediately made friends with a boy of the same age in his class. They had first met at Miles' house in Torquay before term started, my mother having arranged to buy a second-hand blazer from Miles' mother Myriam, while we were still in Spain. It was a wonderfully lucky meeting, because Myriam was one of those rare people you like immediately and I am delighted to say we became firm friends with her, her husband Mike and their daughter Hilary – as we still remain thirty-six years later.

In April we held a fancy dress party for Rory's seventh birthday, all his classmates were invited and Rory was delighted at the variety of costumes which included a cowgirl, an astronaut and a Superman. Rory wore his Arabian costume which I had made for the Nativity play in Jávea, improved by my mother who had removed the staples and machine stitched the seems; fortunately I had just enough duvet cover material left to make a matching costume for two year-old Miranda. We arranged for a couple of young actors from Totnes to create a puppet show performance in the sitting room. The story they enacted was a version of Robin Hood, which of course included the evil Sheriff of Nottingham as the villain of the piece. This gave me a brilliant idea.

In the final robbery from the finca, when the thieves had taken all the clothes we had carefully packed for our month's summer holiday in England, one of Rory's two favourite toys, a racoon glove puppet called Rastus, had also been taken. He was in tears and I didn't know how to comfort him. As soon as he was back in England he had told his grandparents about the loss of Rastus, whereupon my mother immediately went to the toyshop at Dartington where we had originally found the glove puppet and bought an identical replacement. I then hatched a plan with the puppeteers, who would magically produce Rastus at the end of the story – he having escaped from his captors and found his way back to England.

I can still see the look on Rory's face as Rastus appeared in the puppet theatre and the puppeteers asked Rory to come forward to take him. Rory at seven was bright as a button, so I was never totally sure if he believed it was the same toy or whether we had tried to pull the wool over his eyes. If he had doubts he was kind enough not to tell us. (I hope when he reads this, aged 42, he won't be too disappointed!). Snoopy, Rastus 2, Miranda's Jofish and Harrods teddy bear are safely stored together and await the next generation of Chaplins to love them.

Rory and his friend Miles shared a love of contraptions or

inventions and were always trying to make impossible things such as perpetual motion machines or rockets powered by baking powder and a bicycle pump. One Saturday they were playing in the garden and I was upstairs when I looked out of a window and noticed it had begun to rain. When I couldn't see the boys I opened the window and called to them to come inside. Two heads appeared from beneath the back of our Range Rover.

"We're not getting wet Mummy," Rory called up to me. "We've made a hot air balloon and were trying to light the candle, but the matches wouldn't work in the rain so we're doing it under the car."

"DON'T TRY AGAIN!" I yelled.

"JEREMY!" I screamed over the bannisters, "*Get the boys out from under the car ... they're trying to light matches!*"

I heard the door fly open and watched Jeremy sprint across to the drive where he snatched the matches from the boys' hands. At the time our Range Rover, being the best of British and almost new, had just developed a crack in its fuel tank that was weeping pools of petrol onto the tarmac. A tragedy of epic proportions had been averted, as would many more – if not all – during the years that followed.

By the time the blackberries ripened on the hedgerows the following year and the swallows lined up on the telegraph wires preparing for their migration to Africa for the winter, we had settled comfortably and happily into life in this charming Devonshire village. Rory and Miles were about to start their first term at Wolborough and Miranda and Amy would be classmates at a small private school nearby. Our family were once again settled, or so it seemed, but the temptation of a once in a lifetime opportunity, in the form of a beautiful manor house in need of loving owners, would soon be upon us.

Another eight years would pass before the irresistible lure of Greece drew us once more to her shores. This time I was determined to get my own way and take my family to the warm and sunny island, set in a sparkling sea, that I had first read about in my school library when I was thirteen – CORFU!

YOU CAN READ ABOUT HER FAMILY'S FURTHER
ADVENTURES IN JANI'S CORFU TRILOGY.

Apricot Chutney

Makes approx 3 kilos

1½ kilos fresh ripe apricots – stoned and chopped or minced (or strained tinned apricots if you are not in Spain). I found it much easier to stone the fresh apricots after cooking them gently in a little water until soft.

250gms stoned dates or raisins – chopped or minced

1 small tin of prunes, stoned and chopped or minced, plus juice

600ml malt vinegar

750gms Demerera sugar

1 desertspoon powdered ginger

1 tablespoon mustard seed

2 tablespoons coarse sea salt

3 large cloves garlic, crushed

1 large onion, chopped

¼ teaspoon chilli powder

¼ teaspoon paprika

1 teaspoon cinnamon

Small glass brandy

Put all ingredients into a heavy based pan. Bring to boiling point and simmer very gently for at least 3 hours for fresh apricots, about 1½ hours for tinned fruit.

Stir regularly with wooden spoon.

As my family like a smooth chutney I put it all into my food processor immediately after cooking and whizz, but you can blend to suit your preference.

Pour into hot jars, cover and seal with jam pot covers.

The flavour improves with keeping.